The Queen: Or, the Excellency of Her Sex

John Ford, Alexander Goughe, Willy Bang

Materialien zur Kunde

des

älteren Englischen Dramas

Materialien zur Kunde

des älteren

Englischen Dramas

UNTER MITWIRKUNG DER HERREN

F. S. Boas-Belfast, A. Brandl-Berlin, R. Brotanek-Wien, F. I. Carpenter-Chicago, G. B. Churchill-Amherst, Ch. Crawford-London, W. Creizenach-Krakau, E. Eckhardt-Freiburg i. B., A. Feuillerat-Rennes, R. Fischer-Innsbruck, W. W. Greg-London, F. Holthausen-Kiel, J. Hoops-Heidelberg, W. Keller-Jena, R. B. Mc Kerrow-London, G. L. Kittredge-Cambridge, Mass., E. Koeppel-Strassburg, H. Logeman-Gent, J. M. Manly-Chicago, G. Sarrazin-Breslau, L. Proescholdt-Friedrichsdorf, A. Schröer-Cöln, G. C. Moore Smith-Shefeield, G. Gregory Smith-Edinburg, A. E. H. Swaen-Groningen, A. H. Thorndike-Evanston, Ill., A. Wagner-Halle a. S.

BEGRUENDET UND HERAUSGEGEBEN

VON

W. Bang

o. ö. Professor der Englischen Philologie an der Universität Louvain

DREIZEHNTER BAND

LOUVAIN
A. UYSTPRUYST

LEIPZIG
O. HARRASSOWITZ

LONDON
David NUTT

1906

THE

QUEEN

OR THE EXCELLENCY

OF HER SEX

NACH DER QUARTO 1653 IN NEUDRUCK HERAUSGEGEBEN

VON

W. Bang.

LOUVAIN
A. UYSTPRUYST

LEIPZIG   LONDON
O. HARRASSOWITZ   DAVID NUTT

1906

VORWORT.

Tu prima voluptas,
Tu postrema mihi.   Claud.

Als ich als blutjunger Gymnasiast zum ersten Male Forde's *Perkin Warbeck* und *Giovanni und Annabella* in Bodenstedt's Übersetzung las, war der Eindruck ein so nachhaltiger, dass ich später oft und gern zu Forde zurückgekehrt bin.

Zum menschlichen und poetischen Interesse gesellte sich ein philologisches als ich durch meine Vorliebe für Dekker — er ist ein « sonniger Mensch » in der That — dazu veranlasst wurde, die von ihm und Forde gemeinsam verfassten Dramen auf die Teile hin zu untersuchen, die auf den einen oder auf den andern zurückzuführen sind.

So ist mir Jacke's Stimme so vertraut geworden, wie die eines guten Freundes, und als ich sie in der *Queene* wiederzuerkennen glaubte, warf ich mich ihm mit altem Feuer in die Arme : vorsichtiger wäre es vielleicht gewesen, nur höflich den Hut zu lüften ! Das mögen andere, intimere Freunde Forde's entscheiden.

W. B.

VORBEMERKUNGEN.

§ 1. ALEXANDER GOUGHE. Die in mehr als einer Hinsicht interessante Tragi-comoedie, die in den folgenden Blättern zum zweiten Male ein verspätetes Erstehn feiert, teilte das Schicksal von Beaumont und Fletchers *The Wild-Goose Chase* und anderer Stücke bis sie im Jahre 1653 von A. Goughe herausgegeben wurde. Da dieser tätige Praematerialist nicht ins DNB aufgenommen worden ist, so möge uns der folg. Auszug aus Wright's *Historia Histrionica* (Arber, *English Garner*, II, p. 277) über ihn und die Gründe, die ihn zur Herausgabe veranlassten, belehren [1]:

Afterwards, in Oliver's time, they used to Act privately three or four miles or more out of town, now here, now there; sometimes in noblemen's houses, in particular Holland House at Kensington : where the nobility and gentry who met, but in no great numbers, used to make a sum for them ; each giving a broad piece or the like. And ALEXANDER GOFFE, the Woman Actor [2] at Blackfriars, who had made himself known to persons of Quality, used to be the jackal, and give notice of time and place..... Some picked up a little money by publishing copies of plays never before printed, but kept in manuscript *etc.*

Von Stücken, die Goughe so herausgegeben hat, sind mir bekannt : *The Widow*, 1652 (cf. Bullen's Middleton, V, p. 117 ff.), und Carlell's *The Passionate Lovers*, 1655 [3] ; zwischen beide schiebt sich *The Queene*.

§ 2. VERFASSER. Trotz der Abwesenheit jeglicher äusserer Zeugnisse schreibe ich unser anonym überliefertes Drama mit ziemlicher Zuversichtlichkeit John Forde zu. Meine Gründe sind die folgenden : Auf beiden Seiten werden die herr-

---

[1] Einige uns hier nicht interessierende Angaben siehe bei Collier, *Memoirs of the Principal Actors in the Plays of Shakespeare* (Shak. Soc. Publ.), pp. 265 ff.

[2] Er spielte die Rolle der Acanthe, a Maid of Honour, in Massinger's *Picture*, Caenis, Vespasian's Concubine, in desselben *Roman Actor*, sowie nicht näher bestimmte Rollen in Forde's *The Lover's Melancholy* und in Beaumont und Fletcher's Stücken; siehe Folio 1.

[3] Da die Widmung dieses Stückes *To the Illustrious Princess, Mary Dutchess of Richmond and Lennox* für die Biographie Goughe's von Wert ist, so gebe ich sie hier : Madame I humbly offer Your Grace the last sacrifice of this nature that is in my power, having only a hope that it may be receiv'd by you with that favour as when it was formerly presented. And so, Madam, I only dare to appear in an address to you, as others to their Altars, who by sacrifices get pardon for their defects, if not advance their devotions. This was to your Sex indeed a peculiar offering, whilst all either gave as much Passion to their Adorers, or wisht their Beauties great enough to do it : your Graces excellencies alone have been by all admirers esteem'd at so great and just a value, as to create, and not reward mens passions. This with as just a reverence I present to you, hoping for this Romantique passion such an entertainment as none durst expect for real ones ; your severity would deny a reception to those, which your charity may grant to this : And believe, he that attempts all way to express his respects and duty, has more then Fortune will give him leave to shew, The unhappy condition at this time of

MADAM,
*The most humble of all
your Graces most ob-
liged Servants,*
ALEX. GOUGHE.

lichsten Charactere durch das gemeinste Gelichter in ihrer Wirkung geradezu erdrückt — das ist Forde. Auf beiden Seiten constatieren wir ferner ein Nebeneinander moralisch und poetisch hocherhabener Stellen und solcher, die durch rohe Takt- und Geschmacklosigkeiten und den niedrigsten « Humor » entstellt werden — das ist wieder Forde. Sodann ist die Characterzeichnung hüben und drüben dieselbe, ja, ich stehe nicht an zu behaupten, dass ein guter Kenner Forde's in fast allen Personen der *Queene* alte Bekannte wiederzuerkennen glauben wird. Und schliesslich weist der ganze Ideenkreis, die oft gesuchte, fast immer übertrieben hyperbelreiche Ausdrucksweise sowie der ganze Wortschatz des Verfassers der *Queene* entschieden auf John Forde.

Indem ich die Detailarbeit der Dissertation eines Hörers überlasse, verweise ich hier kurz auf die in den Erläuterungen enthaltenen Parallelen, bitte aber die Kritik, sich nicht an diese sondern an Forde selbst halten zu wollen. Er, der Vielgeschmähte [1]), wird's dem Leser dankbar lohnen, dass er sich ihm nähert und um die Ehre näherer Bekanntschaft bittet. Mir selbst wäre es — im Interesse Forde's natürlich — eine wahre Freude, wenn Kate Gordon und Eroclea der anmutigen Königin von Aragonien zum Schwesterkuss die Wange bieten dürften.

§ 3. ABFASSUNGSZEIT. Wie die übrigen Stücke Forde's so enthält auch die *Queene* m. W. keine Anspielung oder dergleichen, die uns erlaubte, das Drama auch nur mit annähernder Bestimmtheit zu datieren (vergl. immerhin Anm. zu Charles his wayn 1788).

Ein *terminus a quo* wird sich vielleicht ergeben, wenn der Einfluss von Burton's *Anatomy of Melancholy* (1621) auf Forde's sämmtliche Dramen einmal untersucht worden ist.

Bei der vollständigen Abwesenheit von Vorarbeiten über Forde's Sprache [2]) und Technik wäre es heute tollkühn, dem Problem mit inneren Gründen näherkommen zu wollen. Den metrical tests *allein* stehe ich im Allgemeinen recht skeptisch gegenüber ; bei Forde aber um so mehr, als sie Hannemann in seinen *Metrischen Untersuchungen zu John Ford*, Halle 1888, pp. 37-38, dazu veranlasst haben, zwei so eminent Forde'sche Stücke wie *'Tis Pity* und *Love's Sacrifice* nur teilweise unserem Dichter zuzuschreiben.

Ich habe das Gefühl, dass *The Queene* zeitlich *The Broken Heart* und *Love's Sacrifice* nahesteht, hebe aber ausdrücklich hervor, dass mein Gefühl nicht massgebend sein kann.

---

[1]) Dass es nicht immer so gewesen ist geht aus dem bisher unbekannt gebliebenen Epigramm hervor, das ich in *Wits Recreation*, 1640 (Repr. Hotten, p. 13), finde :

If e're the Muses did admire that well
Of Helicon, as elder times do tell,
I dare presume to say upon my word,
They much more pleasure take in thee, rare *Ford*.

[2]) Forde's Orthographie habe ich bis jetzt wenigstens in meinen QQ von *Love's Sacrifice* (1633) und *Perkin Warbeck* (1634) mit derjenigen der *Queene* vergleichen können und eine bemerkenswerte Übereinstimmung gefunden. Dagegen weist die Q 1638 von *The Fancies* — ich verdanke deren Kenntniss der liebenswürdigen Zuvorkommenheit des Mr. Bertram Dobell in London — eine Orthographie auf, die sich mit derjenigen der drei genannten QQ nicht deckt. In der Q 1629 von *The Lover's Melancholy* dagegen kommen z. B. die Formen d'ee   do ye, t'ee = to ye wieder fast auf jeder Seite vor (z. B. p. 78 : apply'd t'ee ; cf. dazu Dyce's Anm. I, p. 96 ; « remarkably harsh » mag heute richtig sein, aber Forde'sch *ist* diese Zusammenziehung). — Ebenso wenig wie *The Queene* sind übrigens die alten mir bekannten QQ von Forde'schen Stücken in Scenen eingeteilt.

§ 4. Quellen. Zu der Quellenfrage muss es hier genügen für Haupt- und Nebenhandlung auf Koeppel's *Studien über Shakespeare's Wirkung auf zeitgenössische Dramatiker (Mat. IX)* pp. 70 ff. und auf desselben *Studien zur Gesch. der Ital. Novelle* etc. pp. 95-96 ; 96-97 hinzuweisen. Dass dem Verfasser der *Queene* das viel ältere Stück *The Dumb Knight* — vergl. den handschriftlichen Eintrag auf A 4^v meines Exemplars — unbekannt gewesen wäre, will ich nicht behaupten, doch lässt sich das Gegenteil auch nicht bestimmt erweisen ; dasselbe gilt von Beaumont und Fletcher's *The Woman Hater* : einige schwache Anklänge an *The Queene* finden sich in beiden Stücken, doch sind sie nicht dazu angethan, die Abhängigkeit des jüngeren Dichters darzuthun.

§ 5. Ausgaben. Seit dem Jahre 1653 ist *The Queene* nicht wieder gedruckt worden. Der vorliegende Neudruck beruht auf einem in meinem Besitz befindlichen Exemplar der Originalquarto. Da die für diese verwendeten Typen von augenmörderischer Kleinheit sind, so haben wir einen grösseren Character gewählt, wodurch die Seitengrösse von 11 × 17 cm. auf die gegenwärtigen Verhältnisse verschoben wurde.

Durch Greg's Güte konnte ich sein Exemplar der alten Quarto während der ganzen Dauer der Drucklegung benutzen, wofür ihm an dieser Stelle mein herzlicher Dank gesagt sei. In l. 3693 ist in Greg's Exemplar in dem verderbten hut das h ganz verschwunden ; in l. 3711-12 ist in perilous das u umgekehrt : perilons.

Bei der Drucklegung hat mich Dr. J. Van de Wyer mit scharfem Auge und liebevoller Sorgfalt unterstützt, sodass ich jetzt bei der letzten Collation mit Forde sagen kann :

> We have compar'd the Copie with th' Originall,
> And finde no disagreement !   *The Fancies*, 1638, p. 61.

THE
QUEEN,
OR THE
EXCELLENCY
OF HER
SEX.

An Excellent old Play.

Found out by a Perſon of Honour, and given to the Publiſher,
ALEXANDER GOUGHE.

Αὖθις ἔτ' ἄλλο τέταρτον ἐπὶ χθονὶ πελυβοτείρη,
Ζεὺς Κρονίδης ποίησε διχαιότερον, κὴ ἄρειον
Ἡρωίασων θεῖον γέν⊙, αἳ χαλέονται
Ἡμίθεαι.   Heſiod: lib: 1.

———— Cedat jam Graia vetuſtas
Peltatas mirata Nurus, jam Volſca Camillas
Cedat, & Aſſyrias qua fœmina flectit habenas
Fama tace, Majore cano ————

LONDON,
Printed by *T. N.* for *Thomas Heath*, in *Ruſſel* Street, Neer
the *Piazza* of Covent-Garden, 1653.

TO THE
VERTUOUSLY NOBLE AND
TRULY HONORABLE LADY,
The Lady
₅CATHERINE MOHUN,
Wife to the Lord *Warwick Mohun*, Baron of
Okehampton, my highly honored LORD.

May it please your Ladiship,

M

Adam, Imbolden'd by your ac-
customed candor and unmerited
favours to things of the like
nature, though disproportion'd
worth : (Because this Excellency
seems to contract those perfecti-
₁₅ ons her Sex hath been invested with, which are
as essential to your Ladiship, as light to the Sun)
I presumed to secure this innocent Orphan from
the Thunder-shocks of the present blasting age,
under the safe protecting wreath of your name ;
₂₀ which (I am confident) the vertues of none can
more justly challenge, then those of your Ladiship ; who alone may seem to quicken the lifeless
Scene, and to demonstrate its possibility ; reducing
Fables into Practicks ; by making as great honour

A 2   visible

The *Epistle* DEDICATORY.

25 visible in the mirror of your dayly practise. Your
pardon, Madam, for daring to offer such adulterate Metals, to so pure a Mine ; for making the
Shadow a present to the Substance; the thoughts of
which was an offence, but the performance, a
30 crime beyond the hopes of pardon.   When my
Fate had cast me on the first, I esteemed my self
unsafe (with the Politian) should I not attempt
the latter, securing one error by soaring at a
greater : but my duller eyes endured not the
35 proof of so glorious a Test, and the waxed jun-
cture of my ill contrived feathers melt me into the
fear of a fall : Therefore (with the most desperate offenders) I cast my self on the mercy of the
Bench ; and since I have so clement a Judge as
40 your self, do not wholly despair of absolution, by
reason my Penetential acknowledgment attones
part of the offence ; and your remission of the
whole will eternally oblige.

MADAM,

45   *The humblest of your*

          Ladiships Servants,

     ALEXANDER GOUGHE.

                    TO

To Mr. *Alexander Goughe* upon his publishing
The excellent Play call'd the *Queen* ;
or the Excellencie of her Sex.

I F *Playes be looking glasses of our lives*
5 *Where dead examples quickning art revives* :
   By which the players dresse themselves, and we
By them may forme a living Imagry
To let those sullied, lie in age in dust
Or break them with pretence of fit and just.
10 *Is a rude cruelty, as if you can*
Put on the christian, and put off the man.
But must all morall handsomnes undoe
And may not be divine and civill too.
What though we dare not say the Poets art
15 *Can save while it delights, please and convert;*
Or that blackfriers we heare which in this age
Fell when it was a church, not when a stage,
Or that the * *Presbiters that once dwelt there,*
Prayed and thriv'd though the playhouse were so near.
20 *Yet this we dare affirme there is more gain*
In seeing men act vice then vertue fain;
And he less tempts a danger that delights
In profest players then close Hypocrites ,
Can there no favour to the scæne be shown
25 *Because* Jack Fletcher *was a Bishops son ,*
Or since that order is condemn'd doe you
Think poets therefore Antichristian too;
Is it unlawfull since the stage is down
To make the press act : where no ladies swoune
30 *At the red coates intrusion : none are strip't;*
No Hystriomastix has the copy whip't
No man d' on Womens cloth's : the guiltles presse
Weares its own innocent garments : its own dresse ,
Such as free nature made it : Let it come
35 *Forth Midwife* Goughe,*securely;and if some*
Like not the make or beautie of the play
Bear witnes to 't and confidently say
Such a relict as once the stage did own ,
Ingenuous Reader, merits to be known.
40

* In the origi-
nall it is Puri-
tans.

R. C.

For Plays.

DO you not Hawke ? Why mayn't we have a Play ?
Both are but recreations.   You'll say
Diseases which have made Physitians dumb,
5 By healthful excercise are overcome.
And Crimes escap'd all other laws, have been
Found out, and punish'd by the curious Scene.
Are Stages hurtful for the ill they teach,
And needless for the good ? Which Pulpits preach :
10 Then sports are hurtful, for the time they lose,
And needless to the good, which labour does.
Permit 'm both; or if you will allow
The minde no Hawke, leave yours, and go to Plough.

EDMOND ROOKWOOD.

To Mr. *Goughe,* upon the publication of the Play, call'd, *The* QUEEN, *or the Excellency of her* SEX.

GOUGHE, *In this little Present you create
5 Your self a Trophee, may become a State* ;
For you that preserve wit, may equally
Be ranck'd with those defend our Liberty ;
And though in this ill treated Scene of sense ,
The general learning is but in pretence ;
10 Or else infus'd like th' Eastern Prophet's Dove,
To whisper us, Religion, Honour, Love;

Yet

Yet the more Generous race of men revives
This Lamp of Knowledge, and like Primitives
In Caves, fearless of Martyrdom, rehearse
15 The almost breathless, now, Dramatick verse.
How in the next age will our Youth lament
The loss of wit, condem'd to banishment.
Wit that the duller rout despise, 'cause they
Miss it in what their zealous Priests display :
20 For Priests in melancholy zeal admit
Onely a grave formality for wit ;
And would have those that govern us comply
And cherish their fallacious tyranny.
But wherein States can no advantage gain,
25 They harmless mirth improperly restrain ;
Since men cannot be naturally call'd free,
If Rulers claim more then securitie.
How happens then this rigour o're the Stage
In this restor'd, free, and licentious age?
30 For Plays are Images of life, and cheat
Men into vertue, and in jest repeat
What they most seriously think ; nor may
We fear lest Manners suffer : every day
Does higher, cunninger, more sin invent
35 Then any Stage did ever represent.
It may indeed shew evil, and affright,
As we prize day by th' ugliness of night.
But in the Theatre men are easier caught,
Then by what is in clamorous pulpits taught.

40   T. C.

Persons of the PLAY.

Queen of Arragon.
Petruchi, *a Young Lord.*
Bufo, *a Captain.*
Pynto, *an Astronomer.* } *Kings Party:*
Muretto.
Velasco, *Queens General.*
Lodovico, *his friend.*
Alphonso, *afterwards King.*
Collumello, } *Counsellors to the Queen.*
Almado,
Herophil, *her Woman.*
Salassa, *widow, Mistriss to* Velasco.
Shaparoon, *her friend.*
Mopas, Velasco's *man.*
Hangman.
Messenger.
Groom.
Officers.

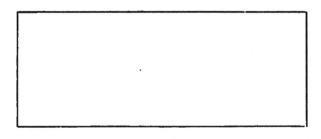

The Queen.

ACTUS PRIMUS.

Enter *Petruchi* with *Bufo*, *Pynto* and
Muretto, in poor habits.

5 *Petr*   LL free, and all forgi-
    A   ven.
        Omnes. Bless her Ma-
        jesty.
        Petr.Henceforth(my
10   friends)take heed how you so hazard
  Your lives and fortunes on the peevish
    motion
  Of every discontent, you will not finde
  Mercy so rife at all times.
15 *Muret*. Gratious Sir *!*
  Your counsel is more like an Oracle,
  Then mans advice, for my part I dare
    speak
  For one, I rather will be rackt asunder
20 Then e're again offend so wise a Ma-
    jesty.
    Petr. 'Tis well, your lives are once
    more made your own ;
  I must attend the execution
25 Of your hot General, each shift now for
    your selves.   *Exit Petruchi*.
  Buf. Is he gone, ha, ha, ha !

We have the common Capony of the
    cleer heavens
Once more o're our heads, Sirs.   30
  Muret. We are at liberty out of the
    Hangmans clutches,
Now,mark,what good language and fair
    words
Will do, Gentlemen.   35
  Pyn. Good language *!* O, let me go
back and be hang'd, rather then live
within the rotten infection of thy Can-
kred breath ; the poison of a flatterers
tongue is a thousand times more dead- 40
ly, then the twinges of a rope ; Thou
birth of an unlucky Planet : .
I abhor thee.
  Muret. Fy, fy ! Can you rail on your
friends thus.   45
  Pyn.Friends,my friend! Captain,come
from that slippery Ele, Captain.
His very cradle was in dirt and mud ;
His milk the oyl of serpents; his mother
a mangy Mermaid, and a male Croco- 50
dile begat him.
  Muret. This needs not sweet, Signior
Pynto.

           B   *Pyn*.

Pyn. Sweet Signior ? Sweet Cog a
55 foyst, go hang thy self, thou'dst jeer the
very rags I wear off my back with thy
fustians of sweet, precious, unmatchable,
rare, wise, juditious, hey do! Pox on
thee ; Sirrah, Sirrah, Hast not thou ma-
60 ny a time and often devoured a whole
table of mine, garnisht with plenty, nay;
variety of good wholesome fare, under
the colour of telling news with a roughy complement ?
65   *Muret.* Good fare of thine !
     Buf. Nay, dear Gentlemen.
     Pyn. Mine ! I mine, Sycophant, I (dost
mark me) to supply thy totters, paund a
whole study of Ephimerides, so rich,
70 that they might have set up a Corporation of Almanack makers; and what had
I in return ? But protestations, (hear-
est thou this maunderer) that I was,
for learning, the soundest ; for bounty,
75 the royallest ; for discourse, the sententioust ; for behavour, the absolutest ; for
all endowments of minde and body, the
most accomplisht that nature ever call'd
her workmanship : but thou dog, thou
80 scoundrel, my beggery was the fruits of
thy flattery. Stand off, Rascal, off.
     Buf. This is excellent 'faith ;
     Muret. How, how ! I flatter ye ?
What thee, thee? A poor lousy uncloakt
85 imposter, a deceitful, couzening, chea-
ting, dull decoying fortune teller ; Thou
pawn books; thou, patcht out of an old
shepheards Calender, that discoursest in
rime of the change of the weather.
90 And whose were thy Ephemerides ?
Why, Impudence, wert thou ever
worth *Erra Pater*'s Prognostication ?
Thou learned ! In what ? By fil-
ching, stealing, borrowing, eating, col-
95 lecting, and counting with as weather-
wise Ideots as thy self ; once in twelve
moneths thou wert indeed delivered,
(like a big bellied wife) of a two penny
Almanack, at *Easter.* A Hospital boy in
100 a blew coat shall transcribe as much in
six hours to serve all the year.
Thou a table of meat, yes, Astrono-
mers fare, air ; or at a feast upon high
holy dayes, three red Sprats in a dish ;
105 that was held gultony too.

I slatter thee ? Thou learned ?
     Pyn. Rascal, Cannibal that feedest up-
on mans flesh.
     Buf. Nay, pray, pray, heartily Gen-
tlemen ; in good earnest, and as I live, 110
and by this hand now——
     Muret. Right thou put'st me in minde
what I should call thee ; Who was't the
cause of all the late insurrection for
which we were all like to be hang'd, 115
and our brave General *Alphonso* is this
day to suffer for ; who but thou, forsooth ; the influences of the Stars, the
conjunction of the Planets, the predi-
ction of the celestial bodies were pe- 120
remptory, that if a' would but attempt
a civil commotion, a' should (I marry
should a') be strait crown'd present
King of *Arragon.* Now your Gipsonly
may i'th moon, your divination hath 125
fairly mounted him ; poor Gentleman,
he's sure to leave his head in pawn for
giving credit to thy prognosticating ig-
norance.
     Pyn. I scorn thee, Parasite.   130
     Muret. You are a stinking starv'd-gut
star-gazer.   Is that flattery or no.
     Buf. 'S foot, What do you mean, Sig-
nior *Pynto*, Signior *Muretto* ?
     Pyn. I will be reveng'd, and watch my 135
time, Sirrah.
     Muret. Do.
     Buf. This is strange my Masters, to
be so neer the place of execution and
prattle so loud ; Come, Signior *Pynto*, in- 140
deed la you shall shake hands.
     Pyn. Let me alone, y'are a foolish
Captain. *Muretto*, I will display thee
for a———
     Muret. Hang thy self, I care not for 145
thee this.
     Buf. Foolish *C*aptain, foolish Captain,
heark ye, *Pynto*, there's no such good
meaning in that word.
     Pyn. A Parrat can eccho, talk to 150
Schollers so.
     Muret. A proper Scholler, stitch up of
waste paper.
     Buf. Sneaks, if I be a fool, I'll bang
out the wits of some of your nodles, or 155
dry bastinado your sides.
Ye *Dogrel*, maungy scabbed owlaglasses,   I'll

I 'll mawle yee, so I will.

160 *Muret.* Captain, sweet Captain, nay, look, now will you put your discretion to coxcombs ?

Buf. Yes, the proudest coxcombs of 'em all, if I be provok'd ; foolish, flesh 165 and blood cannot eudur't.

Muret. So, goodman sky walker, you have made a trim hand on't, to chafe your self into a throat cutting.

Buf. I will shred you both so small, 170 that a very botcher shall shred Spanish needles, with every fillet of your itchy flesh ; call me foolish, ye whelps-moyles; my father was a Corn-cutter, and my mother a muscle woman, 'tis known 175 what I am, and I'll make you know what I am, If my choler be raised but one inch higher.

Pyn. Well, I see *Mars* and *Saturn*, were thy Planets.
180 Thou art a valiant souldier, and there's no dealing with ye. For the Captains sake, I will abate my indignation, *Muretto.* But——

Buf. But i'thy face, I'll have no buts, 185 S' bores, the black guard is more honorably suted then any of us three. Foolish, foolish, will never out of my head whilst I live.

Enter Velasco and Lodovico.

190 *Muret.* Long life, eternal prosperity, the blessing o'th heavens, and honors of the Earth, crown the glorious merits of the incomparable, Captain Don *Velasco.*

195 *Pyn.* The Chime goes again, Captain.

Velas. Who are these poor Creatures, *Lodovico.*

Lodov. My Lord, I know them now, they are some of the late mutineers , 200 whom you (when you, took *Alphonso* prisoner) presented to the rigor of the Law, but since they are by the Queen's pardon set at liberty.

Velas. I should know yonder fel-205 low.

Your name is *Bufo*, if I mistake not.

Buf. My name is my own name, Sir, and *Bufo* is my name, Sir ; if any man shall deny't, I dare challenge him in de-210 fence of my Godfathers that gave me that name, Sir ; and what say you to that, Sir?

Muret. A shallow, unbrain'd, weak, foolish fellow , and so forth : Your 215 lordship understands me ; But for our parts my good Lord——

Velas. Well, Gentlemen, I cannot tell you now, That any poor endeavours of mine own Can work *Alphonso's* peace, yet I have 220 spoke And kneell'd and sued for his reprieve. The Queen Hath heard, but will not grant ; This is 225 the day, And this the time, and place, where he must render The forfeit of his life unto the Law. I onely can be sorry.

Enter Petruchi, *after the hangman* 230 *bearing the axe before* Alphonso, *with Officers.*

Petr. *Alphonso,* here's the place, and this the hour ; Your doom is past, and now the sword 235 of Law Must cut the vein that swell'd with such a frensy Of dangerous blood against your Queen and Country. 240 Prepare your self, 'tis now too late to hope.

Alph. *Petruchi,* what is done I did, my gronnd Was pitty of my country, not malice 245 to't. I sought to free wrack'd *Arragon* from ruin, Which a fond womans government must bring. 250 O had you and the nobles of this land, A touch but of the miseries, her weakness Must force ye of neceessity to feel , You would with me have bent your na-255 ked swords Against this female Mistriss of the Crown, And not have been such children to have fawn'd 260

Upon a girles nodd.

Petr. You are distracted ;
She is our lawful Soveraign, we her
    Subjects.

265 *Alph.* Subjects, *Petruchi,* abjects, and
    so live ;
I come to die, on to the execution.

Pyn. Here's a high Saturnal spirit,
    Captain.

270 *Buf.* Pox o' spirits when they mount
    a man to the Hangmans mercy, I do not
    like such spirits,
Let me rather be a moon calf.

Velas. I come to bid farewel, and in
275   farewel,
To excuse my much ill fortune, for be-
    leeve, Sir,
I hold my victory an overthrow.
To tell you how incessantly I ply'd
280 Her Grace, for your remission, were as
    useless
As was my suit, I sorry for your youth.
Let's part yet reconcil'd.

Alph. With all my heart ;
285 It is my glory, that I was reduc'd
By the best man at arms, that ever
    knighthood
Hath stil'd a Souldier—— Alas ! What
    souls are those ?
290 Now, now, in seeing them I die too late.

Buf. O brave General, O noble Gene-
    ral, we are still the rags of the old Re-
    giment. The truth on't is, we were loth
    to leave thee, till thy head and shoul-
295 ders parted companies. But sweet good
    dear General take courage, what, we
    are all mortal men, and must every one
    pass this way, as simple as we stand
    here.

300 *Alph.* Give me thy hand, farewell; the
    Queen is merciful in sparing you; I have
    not ought to give thee but my last
    thanks.

Buf. Blirt o' giving, our clothes are
305 paid for, and
A day will come shall quit us all.

Alph. Art thou, and thou there too ;
    well, leave thy art,
And do not trust the fixions of the stars,
310 They spoke no truth by me : My Lord
    Velasco,
That creature, there, *Muretto,* is a man

Of honest heart, for my sake take him to
    you :
And now soft, peace to all.   315

Pyn. I will burn my books, forsware
the liberal sciences, and that is my resolution.

Buf. Go thy way for the arrantest
General, that ever led crew of brave 320
Sketdreus.

Petr. Will you make ready, Sir.

Alph. *Petruchi,* yes, I have a debt to
    pay, 'tis natures due.
Fellow before thou ask my pardon, take 325
    it ;
Be sure and speedy in thy fatal blow.

Hangm. Never fear clean shaving, Sir.

Alph. May I have leave to meditate?

Petr. You may.   330

Lodov. A gallant resolution, even in
death.

    Enter Queen, Collummello, Almada,
        Herophil, and attendants.

Col. Stay execution 'tis her Highnes 335
    pleasure ;
Aphonso rise ye, and behold the Queen.

Alph. Beshrew the voice of Majesty,
    my thoughts
Were fixt upon an upper Region now, 340
And traffick not with Earth ; alas great
    woman,
What newer tyranny, what doom, what
    torments
Are borrowed from the conclave of that 345
    hell,
Where legions of worse Devils, then are
    in hell
Keep revels, a proud womans heart.
    What plagues   350
Are broacht from thence to kill me ?

Pyn. The moon is now Lady ⎫
of the ascendant, and the man ⎬ *Aside.*
will dye raving.   ⎭

Alm. Fy, *Alphonso,*   355
Will you commit another strange com-
    motion
With your unruly tongue. And what
    you cannot
Perform in act, attempt to do in words? 360
A dying man be so uncharitable.

Alph. Cry mercy, she is Queen of *Ar-*
    ragon,   And

And would with her own eyes (insteed
365　of maskes
And courtly sports) behold an act of
　death.
Queen, welcom, Queen, here quaff my
　blood like wine ;
370 And live a brave she tyrant.
　　Qu. Alas, poor man.
　　A ph. Poor man, that looks on me, de-
lighted to destroy me.
　　Buf. Good boy i'faith, by this hand a'
375 speaks just as I would do, for all that he
is so near being made puddings meat.
　　Qu. You are sorry
For your late desperate rudeness, Are
you not ?
380　*Alph.* By all my miseries these taunts
　are cruelty.
Worse then the Hangmans ax, I am not
　sorry,
Nay more, will not be sorry, know from
385　me
I hate your sex in general, not you
As y'are a Queen, but as y'are a woman :
Had I a term of life could last for ever,
And you could grant it, yes, and would,
390　yet all
Or more should never reconcile my
　heart
To any she alive-- are ye resolved ?
　　Qu. His spirit flies out in his daring
395　language.
Alphonso though the law require thy
　head ,
Yet I have mercy where I see just cause:
You'l be a new man ?
400　*Alph.* Oh ! A womans tongue
Is sharper then a pointed steel; Tender,
　Madam,
I kiss your Royal hand, and call you
　fair,
405 Assure this noble, this uncovered pre-
　sence,
That richest vertue is your bosoms te-
　nant,
That you are absolutely great and good;
410 I'll flatter all the vices of your sex,
Protesting men are monsters, women
　Angels,
No light ones, but full weighty, natures
　best,
415 I'll proclaim lust a pitty, pride a hand-
　somness.

Deceit ripness of wit, bold scandalous
　scolding ,
A bravery of spirit ; bloody cruelty,
Masculine justice ; more I will maintain 420
That Queens are chief for rule, you
　chief of Queens,
If you'l but give me leave to die in
　peace.
Pray give me leave to die. Pray good 425
　now do,
What think ye, 'tis a Royal grant; hence-
　forth
Heaven be the rest you chose, but never
　come at.　　　　　　　　　　　430
A kinde farewel to all.
　　Col. Can you endure
To let a Rebel prate? off with his head,
And let him then dispute.
　　Petr. I should have us'd　　　　435
The priviledge of time, had I known
　this.
You must not talk so loud.
　　Qu. My Lords, a word :
What if we pardoned him, I think the 440
neerness of his arrival to the stroke of
death,
Will ever be a warning to his Loyalty.
　　Alm. How pardon him ! What means
　your Majesty ?　　　　　　　445
What can you hope from one so wholly
　drown'd
In melancholy and sowre discontent ;
That should he share the Crown, a'
　would imploy't　　　　　　　450
On none but Apes and Flatterers.
　　Velas. Spare, my Lord
Such liberal censure , rather reyn the
　fury
Of Justice, then so spur it on. Great 455
　Mistris,
I will not plead my services, but urge
The glories you may challenge by your
　mercy.
It will be a most sweet becoming act　460
To set you in the Chronicles of memory.
　　Qu. Velasco, thou art not more brave
　in arms
To conquer with thy valour, then thy
　courtesie.　　　　　　　　465
Alphonso, take thy life, who took thee
　prisoner,
Is now become thy spokesman.
　　　　　　　　　　　　Alph.

Alph. Phew, mock not
470 Calamity so grosly.

Velas. You are too desperate :
The Queen hath freely pardoned you.

Qu. And more to purchase kinde opinion of thy Sex, our self will lend our
475 help.   Lords, all your hands.

Lodov. But is the Queen in earnest ?

Velas. It becomes her,
Mercy is God like.

Qu. Officers be gone.   *Exit Officers*
480 Such objects for a Royal presence are
Unfit, here kiss our hand, we dare conceive
That 'twas thy hight of youth, not hate
of us
485 Drew thee to those attempts , and both
we pardon.

Muret. Do not the stars run a wrong
byas now, Signior *Pynto ?*

Pyn. Venus is Lady of the Ascendant,
490 man.   I knew if once he pass the fatal
hour, the influence would work another way.

Muret. Very likely, your reasons are
infallible.
495 *Qu.* What can our favours challenge.

Alph. More true service,
True faith, true Love, then I have words
to utter.

Qu. Which we accept, lead on, here
500 ends this strife,
When Law craves justice, mercy should
grant life.

        Exit all but Pynto and his fellows.

Pyn. Go thy waies for a sure sound
505 brain'd piece whilst thou livest ; *Pynto,*
say I, now, now, now, am I an ass, now my
Masters, hang your selves, 'S foot, I'll
stand to't ; that man whoever he be,
(better or worse, all's one) who is not
510 star wise, is natures fool ; your Astono-
mer hath the heavens, the whole globe
of the earth, and the vast gulf of the
Sea it self, for his proper kingdom, his
fee-simple, his own inheritance , who
515 looks any higher then the top of a stee-
ple, or a may-pool, is worthy to die in
a ditch. But to know the conjuncti-
ons of the Planets, the influences of the
celestial body, the harmony of the
520 spheares, frost and snow, hail and tem-

pests, rain and sun-shine, nay, life and
death ; here's cunning, to be deep in
speculation , to be groping the secrets
of nature.

Muret. O, Sir, there, there, there.   525

Pyn. Let me alone, I say it my self,
I know I am a rare fellow ; why, look,
look ye, we are all made, or let me be
stew'd in Star-shut ; pish, I am confident , and we shall all mount , be- 530
leeve it.

Buf. Shall we , nay, then I am resolv'd.

Muret. Frier *Bacon* was but a brazen
head, in comparison of him.   535

Buf. But why should you not have said
so much before, goodman Jolthead ?

Muret. Nay , look ye , Captain ,
there's a time for all things.

Buf. For all this , what will become 540
of us ; is the sign lucky to venture
the begging of a cast sute ? Let me be
resolved of that once.

Muret. 'Twas wisely urg'd, Captain.

Pyn. Mans richest ornament is his na- 545
kedness , Gentlemen , variety of clo-
thing is the surquedry of fools ; wise men
have their proper solace in the linings
of their mindes ; as for fashions, 'tis a
disease for a horse.   550

Muret. Never richer stuff came from
man.

Buf. 'Zookes, 'tis a scurvy, a pocky, and
a naked answer ; a plague of all your
sentences , whilst I am like to starve 555
with hunger and cold,

        Enter Messenger.

Mes. By your leave, Gentlemen, the
Lord *Alphonso* hath sent you this purse
of gold, commands ye to put your selves 560
into costly sutes, and repair to Court;

All. How ! To Court !

Mes. Where you may happily see him
Crowned King, for that's the common
report ; I was charg'd to urge you to 565
be very speedy : farewel, Gentlemen.
                            Exit.

Pyn. What think ye now, my hearts
of gold ?

Muret. Hearts of gold indeed now, 570
Signior.

                            Pyn.

Pyn. Pish, I am a coxcomb, I ; Oh, the divinity of——

Buf. Bawll no more the weather's
575 cold, I must have utensicles , tollow your leader, ho.　　　　*Exit all.*

Enter Velasco and Lodovico
Velas. Prethee perswade me not.
Lodov. You'l loose your honor.
580 *Velas.* Ide rather loose my honor then my faith :

O, *Lodovico,* thou art witness with me, that I have sworn, and pledg'd my heart, my truth to her deserving memory ,
585 whose beauty, is through the world unfellowed.

Lodov. Here the wisdom of sword men, They deal all by strength not policy.

What exercise shall be fain'd , let me
590 know that ?

Velas. Excuse, why, *Lodovico,* I am sick, And I am sick indeed, sick to the soul.

Lodov. For a decay'd tilter, or a known Coward , this were tollerable
595 now : But to the business ; I have solicited your widow.

Velas. Will she nor speak with me ?

Lodov. Young widows, and grave old Ones two, by your leave care not so
600 much for talking ; if you come once to them you must do, and do, and do again, Again, and again, all's two little, you'l finde it.

Velas. Come, friend, you mock my mi-
605 series.

Lodov. It's a fine laughing matter when the best and most approved souldier of the world , should be so heartsick for love of a placket : Well I have
610 sent your wise servant (for fools are best to be trusted in womens things) to my couzen *Shaparoon,* and by him your second letter, you shall shortly hear what news : My couzen is excellently traded
615 in these mottal businesses of flesh and blood, and will hardly come of with two denials.

Valas. If she prevail, *Lodovico*——

Lodov. What then ? Ply your occu-
620 pation when you come to't, 'tis a fit season of the year, women are hony moon if a man could jump with them at the instant, and prick 'em in the right vain ; else this Queen would never haue sav'd a Traytor from the block , and sudden- 625 ly made him her King and Husband. But no more of that , there's danger in't ; Y'are sick you say ?

Velas. Pierc't through with fiery darts, much worse then death.　　　　630

Lodov. Why your onely present remedy is, then as soon as you can , to quench those fires in the watry Channels of qualification : soft , no more words, behold a prodegy.　　　　635

Florish.
Enter Colonnello , Almada bare , Al-phonso and the Queen Crowned, Hero-phil , Petruchi with a Guard, the King and Queen take 640 their States.

All. Long live *Alphonso* King of Arragon.

Alph. Then we are Soveraign.

Qu. As free, as I by birth :　　　　645
I yeeld to you (my Lord) my Crown, my Heart,
My People, my Obedience; In exchange What I demand is Love.

Alph. You cannot miss it ;　　　　650
There is but one thing that all humane power
Or malice of the Devil could set a broach,
To work on for a breach 'twixt you and 655 me.

Qu. One thing ! Why, is there one thing then, my Lord ?

Alph. Yes, and 'tis onely this ; y'are still a woman.　　　　660

Qu. A woman ! Said you so, sir.

Alph. I confess
You have deserv'd more service, more regard
From me, in my particular, then life 665 Can thank you for ; and that you may conceive
My fair acknowledgment ; although 'tis true,
I might command ; yet I will make a 670 suit ,
An earnest suit t'ee.

　　　　　　　　　Alph.

... that ... hen be granted.

... That ... redeem a while some se-
... thoughts

... I esteem i your sex. You'l
... married

... married batchelor one sennight.

... cannot ... conceive.

... the work.

... as my Lord, this needs no pub-
... declaration.

... fair Madam, hear me. That our
... hearts be kept

... several roof: that you and I
May not for such a short time, come together.

Qu. I understand you not.

Alp. Your patience, Madam,
You interrupt me, That no message pass
Of commendation, questioning our
healths,

Our sleeps, our actions, or what else be-
longs

To common curtesie, 'twixt friend, and
friend.

You must be pleas'd to grant it, I'll have
t so.

Qu. No message of commends !

Alp. Phew, you demur,

It argues your distrust.

Qu. I am content
The King should be obeyed. Pray heaven all be well.

Alp. Treason, thou wer't he didst con-
stitue me

Lord make me prisoner? wer't in that the
means

To raise me up thus high. I thank thee
for't

I sought to honour thee in a defence
Of the Queens beauty ; but wee'l now
forward.

Conduct your mistris, lead her to the
Court,

... and our Lords will follow, there
I will part ;

So many days absence cannot seem but
short.   *Ex. all.*

Act II

Enter Shaparoon and Mopas.

Shap. And as I said nay pray my
friend be covered the business hath
been soundly followed on my part.   725
Yet again, in good sooth, I cannot abide
you should stand bare before me to so
little purpose.

Mop. Manners is a Jewel Madam and
as for standing bare, I know there is som 730
difference. the putting down of a mans
cap, and the putting down of his bree-
ches before a reverend gentlewoman.

Shap. You speak very properly. there
is a great deal of difference indeed. But 735
to come to the point ; Fy, what a stir
I had to make her to receive the letter,
and when she had received it. to open it,
and then to read it ; nay, to read it again
and again : that as I am a very woman, 740
a man might have wrong my smock
dropping wet, with the pure sweat that
came from my body. Friend. I took such
pains with her. Oh my conscience, to
bear a child at those years would not 745
trouble me half so much as the delivery
of that letter did.

Mop. A man-child of my age perhaps,
Madam, would not.

Shap. Yet that were a sore burthen 750
for one that is not us'd to't, I may tell
you. O these coy girles are such wild
cattel to have dealing with.

Mop. What ancient Madams cannot
do one way, let them do another ; she's 755
a rank Jade that being past the breeder,
cannot kick up her heels, wince, and
cry wee-hee : good examples cannot
chuse from ones elders, but work much
to the purpose, being well ply'd, and in 760
season.

Shap. In season ? True, that's a chief
thing ; yes, I'll assure you my friend, I
am but entring into eight and twen-
ty.   765

Mop. Wants somwhat of that too, I
take it ; *I* warrant ye your mark appears

pears yet to be seen for proof of your age, as plain as when you were but fif-
770 teen.

Shap. Truly, if it were well searcht, I think it does.

Your name is *Mopas*, you told me ?

Mop. *Mopas* my name is, and yours
775 Mádam *Shaparoon* I was told.

Shap. A right Madam born I can assure ye.

Mop. Your Ancestors will speak that, for the *Shaparoons* have ever took place
780 of the best French-hoods in the parish; ever since the first addition.

Shap. All this with a great deal of modesty I must confess. Ud's Pittikins, stand by, aside a little: see where the lady coms;
785 do not appear before you are call'd, in any case : but mark how I will work her like wax.

Enter Salassa reading a letter.

Salas. Your servant in all commands
790 *Velasco.* So, and I am resolved to put ye to the test, servant, for your free fools heart, e're I give you the slip, I warrant ye.

Shap. Your ladyship hath considered
795 the premises e're this time , at full , I hope.

Salas. O, *Shaparoon*, you keep true sentinel, what ? I must give certain answer ; must I not?

800 *Shap.* Nay, Madam, you may chuse, 'tis all in your Ladiships discreet consideration. The sum of all is, that if you shew him not some favour, he is no long lives man.

805 *Salas.* Very well ; how long have you been a factress for such Merchants, *Shaparoon.*

Shap. O my Religion ! I a factress ? I am even well enough serv'd for my good
810 will ; and this is my requital. Factress, quoth you ?

Salas. Come, your intercession shall prevail, which is his letter carrier ?

Mop. At your ladiships service.

815 *Salas.* Your Lord *Velasco* sent you ?

Mop. Most true, sweet madam.

Salas. What place hold you about him ?

Mop. I am his *Drugster*, Madam.

Salas. What Sir ? 820

Mop. Being hard bound with melancholy, I give him a purge, with two or three soluble stools of laughter.

Salas. Belike you are his fool, or his jester. 825

Mop. Jester if you please, but not fool, Madam ; for bables belong to fools, and they are then onely fit for ladies secresies, not for Lords.

Salas. But is he indeed sick of late ? 830

Shap. Alas good heart , I suffer for him.

Enter Lodovico.

Lodov. By your leave lady , without ceremony, you know me, and may guess 835 my errand.

Salas. Yet more trouble , nay, then I shall be hail-shot.

Lodov. To be brief. By the honors of a good name, you are a dry-skinn'd wi- 840 dow, and did not my hast concern the life of the noblest Gentleman in *Europe*, I would as much scorn imployments of this nature to you, as I do a proud woman of your condition. 845

Mop. I marry here's one will thunder her widow-head into flitters : stand to't, Signior, I am your second.

Salas. Sir y'are uncivil to exclaim against a lady in her own house. 850

Lodov. A lady , yet a paraquitto, popingjay, your whole worth lies in your gay out side , and your squawling tongue.
A Wagtail is a glorious fowl in respect 855 of many of ye.
Though most of ye are in nature as very fowl as wagtayles.

Salas. Are such as you the Lord *Velasco's* agents in his hot affection ? 860

Shap. Sweet cousen, *Lodovico*, pray now , the lady is most vertuously resolved.

Mop. Heark ye middle-ag'd countess, do not take anothers tale into your 865 mouth , I have occasion to use you in private , and can finde you work enough my self, a word in your ear.

Salas. I protest, I meant more noble
C   answer

870 answer for his satisfaction , then ever
your railing language shall force from
me.

Lodov. Were I the man that doated
on you, I would take a shorter course
875 with you, then to come humbly whi-
ning to your sweet — — pox of all such ridiculous foppery — — I would — —

Salas. Weep your self to death, and be
chronicled among the regiment of kinde
880 tender hearted souls.

Lodov. Indeed, forsooth, I would not;
what, for a widdow one that hath jumpt
the old moyles trot, so oft, that the sci-
atica founders her yet in both her
885 thighs.

Salas. You abuse me grosly.

Lodov. One that hath been so often
drunk with satiety of pleasure, that four-
teen husbands are but as half a draught
890 to quench her thurst in an afternoon.

Salas. I will no longer endure ye.

Lodov. For you, you ? That are neither noble, wise , rich, fair , nor wel-
favoured. For you ?

895 *Mop*: You are all these , if you can
keep your own counsel and let no body
know, Mistris Madam.

Shap. Nay I am so perswaded, and assure your self no body shall know.

900 *Lodov.* Yet forsooth, must you be the
onely precious piece the Lord *Velasco*
must adore, must dye for. But I vow,
if he do miscarry, (as I fear he cannot
recover.)

905 *Salas.* Goodness forbid, Alas ! Is he
sick, sir ?

Lodov. Excellent dissimulation *!* Yes
sure, he is sick, and an everlasting silence
strike you dumb that are the cause on't.
910 But, as I said, if he do go the wrong
way , as I love vertue , your ladiship
shall be ballated through all Christen-
dom, and sung to sciroy tunes, and your
picture drawn over every ballad, sucking
915 of rotten eggs among wheasels.

Salas. Pray give me leave ; Is Lord
Velasco sick ? And lies there ought in me
to comfort, or recover him ?

Lodov. Marry does there, the more In-
920 fidel he *:* And what of all this now *?*

Salas. What would you have me do ?

Lodov. 'Wonders, either go and visi
him, or admit him to visit you ; these
are mighty favours are they not ?

Salas. Why, good Sir, I will grant the 925
later willingly ; he shall be kindly welcom.

Lodov. And laught at while he is here:
shall a not *?*

Salas. What would you have me say ? 930
My best entertainment shall be open to
him ; *I* will discourse to him freely, if
he requires it privately *:* I will be all
what in honour I should.

Lodov. Certifie him so much by letter. 935

Salas. That cannot stand with my modesty , my word and truth shall be my
gage.

Lodov. Enough, do this, and by this
hand I'll ask you pardon for my rude- 940
ness, and ever heartily honour you.

Mop. I shall hear from you when my
leasures serves.

Shap. Most assuredly. Good destines
speed your journey.   945

Mop. All happiness ride ever before
you, your disgraces behinde you, and
and full pleasure in the midst of ye.
                                Exeunt.

Enter Bufo in fresh apparel, ushering 950
        Herophil.

Her. My over kinde, Captain, what
would you say ?

Buf. Why, Mistris, I would say, as a
man might say forsooth, indeed I would 955
say.

Her. What, Captain ?

Buf. Even whatsoever you would
have me to say, forsooth.

Her. If that be all, pray say nothing. 960

Buf. Why look ye, Mistris, all what *I*
say if you mark it well, is just nothing ;
As for example , To tell you that you
are fair, is nothing, for you know it
your self ; to say you were honest, were 965
an indignity to your beauty, and upon
the matter nothing, for honesty in a fair
woman is as good as nothing.

Her. That is somwhat strange to be
proved.   970

Buf. To a good wit, dear Mistris, nothing's impossible.

                      Her. Sure

Her. Sure the Court and your new clothes have infected you. Would *I* were a purse of gold, for your sake, Captain, to reward your wit.

Buf. I would you were, mistris, so you were not counterfeit metal, I should soon try you on the too true touchstone of my affections, indeed forsooth.

Her. Well, witty Captain, for your love I must pass away in debt, but will not fail to think on't. But now I am in hast.

Buf. If you would but grant me but one poor request, before you go, I should soon dispatch and part.

Her. Name it, Captain.

Buf. Truly, and as I live, 'tis a very small triffle for your part, all things considered.

Her. But cannot you tell what it is?

Buf. That were a fine jest indeed, why, I would desire, intreat, and beseech you.

Her. What to do?

Buf. There you have it, and thank you too.

Her. I understand you not.

Buf. Why, To do with you, forsooth, to do with you.

Her. To do what?

Buf. In plain words, I would commit with you, or as the more learned phrase it, if you be pleased to consent, I would ravish you.

Her. Fy, fy, Captain, so uncivil, you made me blush.

Buf. Do I say; why, I am glad I have it for you : Souldiers are hot upon service, mistris, and a wise mans bolt is soon shot ; as the proverb says:

Her. Good Captain, keep up your bolt till I am at leasure to stand fair for your mark. If the Court Stalions prove all so rank, I will vow all to ride henceforth upon an ass ; so, Captain, I must leave you.   *Exit Herophil.*

Buf. Fare-wel heartily to you forsooth.

Go thy waies for as true a Mistris as ever fowled clean Napary. This same whorson Court diet, cost, lodging, change of clothes, and ease, have addicted me villanously to the itch of concupiscence.

Enter Alphonso ; Pynto and Muretto complementing on either side of him.

Alph. They all shall not intreat me.

Muret. Your Majesty were no King, if your own will were not your own law.

Pyn. Always, my Lord, observing the domination of the Planets : As if *Mars* and *Venus* being in conjunction, and their influence working upon your frailty ; then in any case you must not resist the motion of the celestial bodies.

Muret. All which (most gracious Soverain) this most famous Scoller will at a minute foretel.

Buf. All hail to the King himself, my very good Liege, Lord, and most gratious benefactor.

Alph. What need I other counsellors then these.
Shall I be forc't to be a womans slave ?
That may live free, and hate their fickle sex.

Muret. O 'tis a glorious vertue in so magnificent a Prince to abstain from the sensual surfets of fleshly and wanton appetites.

Alph. I finde the inclination of such follies.
Why, what are women?

Buf. Very pleasant pretty necessary toys, an't please your Majesty ; I my self could pass the time with them, as occasion migh serve, eight and forty hours out right, one to one alwaies provided.

Pyn. Yet of all the seven planets, there are but two women among them, and one of them two is chast, which is as good as if shee were a boy.

Muret. That is not to be questioned ; the best of women are but troubles and vexations, 'tis man that retains all true perfection, and of all men your Majesty.

Enter Almada and Collummello.

Alph. Ye are to rude to enter on our privacies,

C 2   with

1075 without our license, speak, your business Lords.

    Alm. We came from your most vertu-
ous Queen.

    Alph. No more.

1080   *Col.* A month is well nigh past , and
yet you slack

Your love to her : What mean you, sir,
so strangely

To slight a wife whose griefs grow now
1085   too high,

For womanhood to suffer.

    Alm. Is't your pleasure

To admit her to your bosom ?

    Alph. Y'are too sawcy.

1090 Return, and quickly too, and tell her
thus ;

If she intend to keep her in our favour,
Let us not see her.

    Col. Say you so, Great Sir;

1095 You speak it but for tryal

    All. Ha, ha, ha.

    Col. O, Sir, remember what you are ,
and let not

The insinuations of these servile crea-
1100   tures,

Made onely men by you, sooth and tra-
duce

Your safety to a known and willful
danger.

1105 Fix in your thoughts the ruine you have
scap't ;

Who freed you ; who hath rais'd you to
this height,

And you will then awake your judg-
1110   ments eye :

The Commons murmur, and the streets
are fill'd

With busie whispers : Yet in time recal
Your violence.

1115   *Alph.* As I am King, the tongue

Forfeits his head that speaks another
word.

    Muretto, Talk we not now like a King ?

    Muret. Like one that hath the whole
1120 World for his proper Monarchy , and it
becomes you Royally.

    Enter Queen, Petruchi, and Herophil.

    Buf. The Queen, and my Mistris ; O
brave, we shall have some doings hard
1125 to hand now , I hope.

    Alph. What means the woman ? Ha !
Is this the duty

Of a good wife, we sent not for you, did
we ?

    Qu. The more my duty that I came 1130
unsent for ;

Wherein my gratious Lord have I of-
fended ?

Wherein have I transgrest against thy
laws   1135

O sacred Marriage ? To be sequestred
In the first spring and *April* of my joys
From you, much dearer to me, then my
life ?

By all the honour of a spotless bed,   1140
Shew me my fault.and I will turn away,
And be my own swift executioner.

    Alph. I take that word. Know then
you married me

Against my will, and that's your fault   1145

    Qu. Alas ! Against your will ? I dare
not contradict

What you are pleased to urge. But by
the love

I bare the King of *Arragon,* (an oath   1150
As great as I can swear by) I conceiv'd
Your words to be true speakers of your
heart,

And I am sure they were ; you swore
they were.   1155

How should I but beleeve, that lov'd so
dearly ?

    Alph. Come then you are a trifler, for
by this

I know you love me not.   1160

    Qu. Is that your fear ?

Why la now, Lords, I told you that the
King

Made our division but a proof of faith.

Kinde husband, now I'm bold to call 1165
you so ;

Was this your cunning to be jealous of
me

So soon ? We women are fine fools
To search mens pretty subtilties.   1170

    Muret. You'l scarce find it so   *Aside.*

    Alph.   She would perswade mee
strangely.

    Qu. Prethee, Sweet heart,

Force not thy self to look so sadly; troth 1175
It sutes not with thy love, 'tis well. Was
this

                        Your

Your sennights respite ? Yet, as I am a
   Queen,
1180 I fear'd you had been in earnest.
   Alph. Earnest : Hence
Monstrous enchantress, by the death I
   owe
To Nature, thou appear'st to me in this
1185 More impudent then impudence, the
   tyde
Of thy luxurious blood is at the full;
And cause thy raging plurisie of lust
Cannot be sated by our royal warmth,
1190 Thou tri'st all cunning petulent charms
   to raise
A wanton devill up in our chast brest.
But we are Canon-proof against the shot
Of all thy arts.
1195   *Qu.* Was't you spoke that, my Lord ?
   Pyn. Phaeton is just over the orb of
the moon, his horses are got loose, and
the heavens begin to grow into a com-
bustion.
1200   *Alph.* I'll sooner dig a dungeon in a
   mole-hill,
And hide my crown there, that both
   fools and children
May trample o're my Royalty, then ever
1205 Lay it beneath an antick womans feet.
Couldst thou transshape thy self into a
   man,
And with it be more excellent then man
Can be ; yet since thou wer't a woman
1210   once,
I would renounce thee.
   Petr. Let the King remember
It is the Queen he speaks too.
   Alph. Pish, I know
1215 She would be well contented but to
   live
Within my presence; not for love to me,
But that she might with safety of her
   honour,
1220 Mix with some hot vein'd letcher, whose
   prone lust
Should feed the rank impostume of de-
   sires,
And get a race of bastards, to whose
1225   birth
I should be thought the Dad. But thou,
   thou woman,
E're I will be the cloak to thy false play,
I'll couple with a witch, a hag ; for if

Thou canst live chast, live by thy sel 1230
   like me.
Or if thou wouldst perswade me that
   thou lov'st me,
See me no more, never. From this time
   forth   1235
I hate thy sex ; of all thy sex, thee worst.
   Exit Alphonso, Bufo, Pynto.
   Alm. Madam, dear Madam, yet
Take comfort, time will work all for the
   best   1240
   Qu. Where must I go ?
   Col. Y'are in your own Kingdom, 'tis
   your birth-right,
We all your Subjects; not a man of us,
But to the utmost of his life, will right 1245
Your wrongs against this most unthank-
   ful King.
   Qu. Away, ye are all Traytors to pro-
   fane
His sacred merits with your bitter terms. 1250
Why, am I not his Wife ? A wife must
   bear
Withal what likes her Lord t'upbraid
   her with,
And yet 'tis no injustice. What was't 1255
   he said ?
That I no more should see him, never,
   never.
There I am quite divorst from all my
   joys,   1260
From all my paradice of life. Not see
   him ?
'Twas too unkinde a task. But he com-
   manded
I cannot but obey. Where's *Herophil* ? 1265
   Her. Here Madam.
   Qu. Go hang my Chamber all with
   mourning black ;
Seal up my windows, let no light survey,
The subtle tapers that must eye my 1270
   griefs.
Get from me Lords, I will defie ye all,
Y'are men, and men (O me) are all un-
   kinde.
Come hither *Herophil*, spread all my 1275
   robes,
My jewels and apparel on the floor,
And for a Crown get me a Willow
   wreath :
No, no, that's not my colour, buy me a 1280
   veil
                            In-

Ingrayn'd in tawny. Alas, I am forsaken,
And none can pitty me.
 Petr. By all the faith
1285 I ow to you my soveraign, if you please
To enjoy me any service, I will prove
Most ready and most true,
 Qu. Why should the King
Despise me? I did never cross his will,
1290 Never gainsaid his, yea; yet sure I fear
He hath some ground for his displeasure.
 Her. None,
Unless because you sav'd him from the
block.
1295 *Qu.* Art thou a pratler too? Peace,
Herophil,
Tempt not a desperate woman. No man
here
Dares do my last commends to him.
1300 *Muret.* If your excellent Majesty
please to repose confidence in me; I will
not onely deliver him your commenda-
tions, but think my self highly dishono-
red, if he return not his back to you by
1305 letter.
 Petr. Off beast, made all of baseness,
do not grieve
Calamity, or as I am a knigh,
I'll cut thy tongue out.
1310 *Muret.* Sweet Signior, I protest——
   Exit Muretto.
 Petr. Madam, beleeve him not, he is a
Parasite;
Yet one the King doth dote on.
1315 *Qu.* Then beshrew ye,
You had not us'd him gently, had I
known't,
I would have kneell'd before him, and
have sent
1320 A handful of my tears unto the King.
Away, my Lords, here is no place to
revel
In our discomfits. *Herophil,* let's hast,
That thou and I may heartily like wi-
1325 dows
Bewail my bridal mockt Virginity.
 Col. Let's follow her my lords; I fear
to late
The King will yet repent these rude di-
1330 visions.   *Exeunt.*
 Enter Velasco, Lodovico, Mopas.
 Lodov. Complement? 'Tis for Bar-
bors shops; know your own worth, you

speak to a frail commodity; and barter't
away roundly, my Lord.   1335
 Velas. She promis'd free discourse?
 Lodov. She did: Are ye answer'd?

 Enter Salassa, Shaparoon.
 Shap. Madam, my Lord *Velasco* is
come, use him nobly and kindly, or—— 1340
I say no more.
 Salas. To a poor widow's house my
Lord is welcom.
Your lordship honours me in this fa-
vor; in what thankful entertainment I 1345
can, I shall strive to deserve it.
 Shap. Your sweet lordship is most
heartily welcom, as I may say.
 Mop. Instead of a letter, Madam good-
face, on my Lord's behalf, I am bold to 1350
salute you.
 Lodov. Madam *Salassa,* not distrusting
the liberty you granted, now you and
my Lord are in you own house, we will
attend yee in the next room; Away, 1355
Couzen; follow, sirrah.
 Shap. It is a woman part to come behinde.
 Mop. But for two men to pass in be-
fore one woman, 'tis too much a con- 1360
science; on reverend antiquity.
  Exit Lodovico, Shaparoon, Mopas.
 Salas. What is your lorships plea-
sure?
 Velas. To rip up   1365
A story of my fate. When by the Queen
I was imploy'd against the late Commo-
tioners,
(Of whom the now King was chief Lea-
der) then   1370
In my return you pleas'd to entertain
me
Here in your house.
 Salas. Much good may it do your
lordship.   1375
 Velas. But then, what conquest gain'd
I by that conquest,
When here mine eyes, and your com-
manding beauty
Made me a prisoner to the truest love, 1380
That ever warm'd a heart.
 Salas. Who might that be?
 Velas. You, Lady, are the deity I
adore,
         Have

1385 Have kneell'd too in my heart, have
vow'd my soul to,
In such a debt of service, that my life
Is tenant to your pleasure.
Salas. Phew, my Lord ;
1390 It is not nobly done to mock me thus.
Velas. Mock you ? Most fair *Salassa*,
if e're truth
Dwelt in a tongue, my words and
thoughts are twins.
1395 *Salas.* You wrong your honor in so
mean a choise.
Can it be though, that that brave man,
Valasco,
Sole Champion of the world, should
1400 look on me?
On me, a poor lone Widow? 'Tis impossible.
Valas. I am poorer
In my performance now, then ever; so
1405 poor,
That vows and protestations want fit
credit
With me to vow the least part of a
service
1410 That might deserve your favour.
Salas. You are serious?
Velas. Lady, I wish that for a present
tryal,
Against the custome of so sweet a na-
1415 ture,
You would be somwhat cruel in com-
mands.
You dare not sift the honor of my
faith
1420 By any strange injunction, which the
speed
Of my glad undertaking should not
cheerfully
Attempt,or perish in the sufferance of it.
1425 *Salas.* You promise Lordly.
Velas. You too much distrust
The constancy of truth.
Salas. It were unnoble,
On your part to demand a gift of
1430 bounty,
More then the freedom of a fair allowance,
Confirm'd by modesty and reason's warrant
1435 Might without blushing yeeld unto.
Velas. Oh, fear not,

For my affections aim at chast contents;
Not at unruly passions of desire.
I onely claim the title of your servant,
The flight of my ambitions soars no 1440
higher,
Then living in your grace, and for in-
couragement
To quicken my attendance now and
then 1445
A kinde unravisht kiss.
Salas. That's but a fee,
Due to a fair deserver : but admit
I grant it, and you have it; may I then
Lay a light burthen on you. 1450
Velas. What is possible
For me to venture on, by how much
more
It carries danger in't; by so much more
My glorie's in the atchievement. 1455
Salas. I must trust ye.
Velas. By all the vertues of a Souldi-
ers nane,
I vow and sware.
Salas. Enough, I take that oath : 1460
And thus my self first do confirm your
warrant.
Velas. I feel new life within me.
Salas. Now be Steward,
For your own store, my lord, and take 1465
possession
Of what you have purchased freely.
Velas. With a joy.
As willing as my wishes can arrive at.
kisses her. 1470
Salas. So, I may claim your oath now.
Velas. I attend it.
Salas. *Velasco*, I do love thee, and am
jealous
Of thy spirit, which is hourly apt 1475
To catch at actions; if I must be Mistris
Of thee and my own will,thou must be
subject
To my improvements.
Velas. 'Tis my souls delight. 1480
Salas. Y'are fam'd the onely fighting
Sir alive ;
But what's this;if you be not safe to me.
Velas. By all — —
Salas. you shall not sware, take heed of 1485
periury.
So much I fear your safety, that I com-
mand,
For

For two years space, you shall not wear a
1490　　sword,
A dagger, or stelletto; shall not fight
On any quarrel be it neer so just.
　　Velas. Lady!
　　Salas. Hear more yet; if you be baffled,
1495 Rail'd at, scorn'd, mock'd struck, baffi'd,
　　kick'd,
　　Velas. (O Lady!)
　　Salas. Spit on, revil'd, challeng'd, pro-
　　vok'd by fools,
1500 Boyes, anticks, cowards.
　　Velas. ('Tis intollerable.)
　　Salas. I charge you (by your oath) not
　　to reply
In word, deed, look: and lastly, I con-
1505　　jure ye
Never to shew the cause to any living
By circumstance or by equivocation;
Nor till two years expire to motion
　　love.
1510　　*Velas.* Why do you play the Tyrant
　　thus?
　　Salas. 'Tis common
T' observe how love hath made a Co-
　　ward valiant;
1515 But that a man as daring as *Velasco*,
Should to express his duty to a Mistris,
Kneel to his own disgraces, and turn
　　Coward,
Belongs to me and to my glories onely;
1520 I'm Empress of this miracle. Your oath
Is past, if you will lose your self you
　　may.
　　How d'ee, Sir?
　　Velas. Woman thou art vain and
1525 cruel.
　　Salas. Wilt please your lordship tast
　　a cup of wine,
Or stay and sup, and take a hard bed
　　here?
1530 Your friends think we have done
　　strange things this while.
Come let us walk like Lovers: I am pit-
　　tiful,
I love no quarrels.
1535　　*Velas.* Triumph in my ruins.
There is no act of folly but is common
In use and practise to a scornsul woman.
　　　　　　　　　　　　　　　　Exeunt.

Act III.

Enter Alphonso, Almada, Muretto,　　1540
　　Bufo, Pynto, and attendants.

　　Alph. You have prevail'd, yet e're you
　　came (my Lord)
Muretto, here this right, right, honest
　　man　　　　　　　　　　　　　　　　1545
Confirm'd me throughly, now to witness
　　further
With what a gratitude I love the
　　Queen.
Reach me a bowle of wine.　　　　　1550
　　Alm. Your Majesty more honors me,
in making me the Messenger of this most
happy concord, then addition of great-
ness can express.
　　Muret. I ever told you,　　　　　1555
How you would his Grace, inclin'd at
　　last
　　Pyn. The very *Jove* of benignity, by
whose gentle aspect the whole sphere of
this Court and Kingdom are (like the 1560
lesser orbes) moved round in the harmony of affability.

　　　　Enter one with wine.
　　Alph. My Lord *Almado*, health unto
　　your Mistris,　　　　　　　　　　　1565
A hearty health, a deep one.
　　Alm. upon my knee
My duty gladly answers　　　*drinks.*
　　Alph. Give him wine.
There's not a man whoever in our 1570
　　Court
(Greater or meaner) but shall pledge
　　this health,
In honor of our Queen, our vertuous
　　Queen.　　　　　　　　　　　　　　1575
Commend us, and report us as you
　　finde.
　　Alm. Great Sir, I shall with joy.
　　Alph. *Bufo* and *Pynto*,
All in, and drink, drink deep, let none 1580
　　be spar'd,
Comers or goers, none.
　　Buf. Away my hearts.
　　Pyn. Wee'll tickle it till the welkin
　　　　　　　　　　　　　　blussle

1585 blussle again, and all the fixt Stars dance the old measures.

Muret. I shall attend to wait upon your lordship to the Caraoch. *Exeunt.*

Manet Alphonso.

1590 *Alph.* So, so, far reaching pollicy, I adore thee,

Will hug thee as my dearling

Shallow fools

Dive not into the pitch of regular Sta-

1595 tists.

Henceforth my Stratagem's of scorn and hatred

Shall kill in smiles. I will not strike and frown,

1600 But laugh and murther.

Enter Muretto.

Alph. Welcom, are we safe?

Muret. Most free from interruption: The Lord *Velasco* is newly entred the

1605 Court; I have given the watch word that they ply him mainly; the conclusion (I know cannot but break off in hurle-burly.

Alph. Good, good, I hate him mortal-

1610 ly. 'Twas he

Slaved me to th'hangmans ax: But now go on;

Petruchi is the man, you say, must stand The Champion of her lust.

1615 *Muret.* There may be yet vertuous in-tention even in bad actions, in lewd words, I urge no further then likely-hoods may inform.

Alph. Phew, that's thy nobleness: But

1620 now *Muretto,*

The eye of luxury speaks loud in si-lence.

Muret. Why look ye, Sir, I must con-fess I observ'd some odd amorous glan-

1625 ces, some sweet familiar courteous toy-ing smiles; a kinde of officious bold-ness in him, Princelike and Queenlike allowance of that boldness in him again; sometimes I might warily overhear her

1630 whispers. But what of all this? There might be no harm meant.

Alph. Fy, no, the grafting of my fore-head, nothing else.

Grafting, grafting, *Muretto,* A most Gen-

1635 tleman-like exercise; a very mystery be-longs to't.

And now and then they walk thus, arm in arm, twist fingers: ha. Would they not *Muretto?*

Muret. 'Tis wondrous fit a great 1640 Queen should be supported, Sir; and for the best lady of 'em all, to discourse familiarly with her supporter, is court-ly and passing innocent.

Alph. She and *Petruchi* did so? 1645

Muret. And at her passing to her pri-vate lodgings, attended onely with her lady in ordinary. *Petruchi* alone went in before her.

Alph. Is't true! Went in before her! 1650 Canst prove that?

Muret. Your Majesty is too quick, too apprehensive of the worst: I meant he perform'd the office of an Usher.

Alph. Guilty apparently: Monstrous 1655 woman! Beast!

Were these the fruits of her dissembling tears!

Her puling, and her heart sighs. But, Muretto, 1660

I will be swift *Muretto,* swift and ter-rible.

Muret. I am such another Coxcomb; O my side too.

Yet faith, let me perswade ye; I hope 1665 your wife is vertuous.

Alph. Vertuous? The Devil she is, 'tis most impossible.

What kiss and toy, wink, prate, yet be vertuous? 1670

Muret. Why not Sir? I think now a woman may lie four or five nights toge-ther with a man, and yet be chast; though that be very hard, yet so long as 'tis possible, such a thing may be. 1675

Alph. I have it, wee'll confer; let's stand aside.

Enter Bufo and another Groom with wine, both drunk; Bufo handing Velasco by the shoulders. 1680

Buf. Not drink more? By this hand you shall drink eleven whole healths, if your cap be wooll or beaver; and that's my resolution.

Gro. 'Sfoot, eleven score, without 1685 dishonor be it spoken to any mans per-son out of this place.

D *Velas.* Prethee,

Velas. Prethee, I can no more, 'tis a
profession
1690 I dare not practice, nay, I will not.

Buf. How will not? Not her Queen-
ships health?
Hark ye, thy stincking and unwholesom
words——
1695 Will not——You will not——You say you
will not?

Velas. I say so, pray be answer'd.

Gro. Pox of all flinchers ; if a' say
a will not,
1700 Let him chuse, like an arrant dry lord
as he is.

Buf. Give me the bowl, I must be valiant.
You, Sirrah, man at arms ; Here's a ca-
1705 rouse
To the King, the Queen, and my self.

Gro. Let't come, I ll have that i'faith,
Sweet, sweet, sweet, Captain.

Buf. Hold, give the lord first, drink it
1710 up lord, do, ump.

Velas. Away I say, I am not in the
tune.

Buf. Tune, tune? 'Sblood, d'ee take
us for fiddlers, scrappers, rime canters by
1715 tune? By this light, I'll scourge ye like
a town top : Look ye, I am urg'd——
Ump——And there's a side blow for ye,
like a sober thing as ye are.

Gro. well done i'faith, precious Cap-
1720 tain.

Velas. Dar'st thou do this to me knowing who I am?

Buf. Yes, in the way of daring, I
dare kick you thus, thus, Sir up and
1725 down.   There's a jolt on the bum too :
How d'ee like it?

Velas. 'Tis well! You use the priviledge of the place.
There was a time the best of all this
1730 Court
Durst not have lift a hand against me
then.
But I must bear it now.

Alph. Is not this strange *Muretto*?

1735 *Muret.* I can scantly credit mine own
eyes : The Captain follows his instructions perfectly.

Buf. Not drink? Mahound, Infidel.
I will fillip thy nose, spit in thy face,

Mungrel ; brave, a Commander, ha?   1740

Velas. O woman—woman—woman.

Buf. That's a lie, a stark one, 'tis
known I nere was a woman in my life.
I am weary beating of him, and can
stand no longer.   *Groom*, kick him thou 1745
up and down in my behalf ; or by this
flesh I'll swinge you, sirrah.

Gro. Come aloft, Jackanapes : come
aloft, sirrah.   *kicks, beates him.*

Alph. Why sure *Velasco* dares not 1750
fight.

Muret. It must be some or other hath
bewitched him.

            Enter Pynto.

Pyn. Avant, I saw twelve dozen of 1755
Cuckolds in the middle region of the
air, galloping on a black Jack, Eastward
ho.   It is certain that every dozen went
for a company, and they are now be-
come a corporation.   *Aries* and *Taurus*, 1760
the Bull and the Ram, two head signs,
shall be henceforth their recognizances,
set up in the grand hall of their politick
convocations———whirr, whirr, there,
there, just under the rainbow ambles 1765
Mercury, the thin bearded thief that
stole away the Drappers wife, while the
good man was made drunk at the Stillyard, at a beaver of Dutch bread and
Renish wine, and lay all night in pure 1770
holland in's stockings and shoes.   Pish,
Talke not to me, I will maintain against
the Universities of both the *Indies*, that
one Aldermans horse is more right wor-
shipful, then any six Constables, brown 1775
bills and all.   Now, now, now, my
brains burn in Sulphur, and thus will I
stalk about, and swim through a whole
Element of dainty, neat, brisk, rich
claret, canary, or maligo.   Am not I 1780
Pynto, have not *I* hiren here? What art
thou, a full moon, or a moon calf?

Buf. No, no, 'tis a dry Stock-fish, that
must be beaten tender.

Velas. Was ever man so much a slave 1785
as *I*?

Pyn. Does *Saturn* wince? Down with
him, let *Charles* his wayn run over his
North pole ; it shall be justified too.

Gro. Now, Sir, having taken a little 1790
breath, have at ye once more, and *I* have
done.   *Enter*

Enter Mopas and Lodovico.

Mop. Clubs, clubs, I have been the
1795 death of two Brewers horses , and two
catch-poles,my self,and now be try'd by
two fools and ten knaves : O monstrous
base,horrible;is my lord past recovery ?

Velas. Hold, prethee, fellow hold, I
1800   have no sword,
Or if I had, I dare not strike again.

Buf. U'ds bones, were ye an invinci-
ble Armado,
Ide pound ye all like brown paper rags.

1805 *Lodov.* Let me be strucken blind ! The
shame of fate ;
Velasco, baffled,and not dare to strike !
Dogs, drunken dogs, I'll whip ye to
your kennels.

1810 *Velas.* Nay good, forbear.
Mop. Bilbo come forth and shew thy
foxes tayl.
Nay, nay, give me liquor, and I'll fight
like a rorer.

1815 *Pyn.* Keep standing ho; the Almanack
says plainly 'tis no season to be let
blood, the sign is mortal. Hold !

Alph. Yes I command. Uncivil ill
bred beasts.

1820 How dares ye turn our pallace to a
booth ?
How dare the proudest of ye all lift up
A hand against the meanest of those
creatures

1825 Whom we do own for ours ? Now,now
you spit
The ancient rancor of you bitter galls
Wherewith you strove to wound us
heretofore.

1830 *Lodov.* We are abus'd, My Lord.
Alph. Fellow, Thou lyest.
Our Royal eyes beheld the pride and
malice
Of thee *Velasco* ; who in hate to us

1835 Deny'st to honour our remembrance,
though
But in a pledg'd health.

Velas. Therein I was wrong'd.
Alph. No, therein all thy cunning
1840   could not hide
The rage of thy malitious heart to us;
Yet know,for tryal of thy love we caus'd
This onset, we will justifie the hight
Of thy disgraces ; what they did was

1845   ours.

Hence Coward, baffled, kickt, despis'd
and spurn'd.

Buf. Hang thy self ; a pox on thee.

Exit Alphonso, Muretto,
Pynto, Bufo, Groom. 1850

Lodov. O y'are undon : What Devil,
Hag, or Witch
Hath stoln your heart away ?

Velas. I cannot tell.

Lodov. Not fight 'tis enough to shame 1855
us all.

Velas. Happy was I, that living liv'd
alone,
Velasco was a man then, now is none.

Exeunt. 1860

Mop. Is't even so,no man now ; then I
smell how things stand : I'll lay my life,
his lady sweet heart hath given him the
Gleek , and he in return hath gelded
himself, and so both lost his courage and 1865
his wits together.   *Exit.*

Enter Queen, Almado, Collumello,
Petruchi and Herophil.

Qu. Speak o're the words again ; and
good my lord   1870
Be sure you speak the same , the very
words ;
Our Queen, our vetuous Queen; Was't
so ?

Alm. Just so ;   1875
And was withal in carriage so most
kinde,
So Princely, that I must do wrong to
gratitude,
In wanting action to express his love.   1880

Qu. I am the happiest she that lives.
Petruchi,
Was I mistook or no? Why good my
lords,
Observe it well. There is a holy league 1885
Confirm'd and ratify'd 'twixt Love and
Fate.
This sacred Matrimonial tye of hearts,
Call'd marriage, has Divinity within't.
Prethee, *Almado,*tell me, smil'd the King 1890
When he commended to me ?

Alm. Madam, yes ;
And affably concluded all in this ;
Commend us, and report us as you find.

Qu. For loves sakes, no man prattle 1895
of distrust.

It shall be treason whosoever says
The King's unkinde. My thinks I am all
    air ,
1900 My soul has wings.
    Petr. And we are all o'rejoy'd
In this sweet reconciliation.
    Qu. Wee'll visit him (my Lords) in
        some rich mask
1905 Of rare device, as thus ; Pish, now I
        think on't,
The world yeelds not variety enough
Of cost, that's worthy of his Royal eyes,
Why *Herophil ?*
1910   *Her.* Here, Madam.
    Qu. Now beshrew me
But I could weep for anger - — If 'twere
    possible
To get a chariot cut out of a rock,
1915 Made all of one whole Diamond, drawn
        all on Pavements
Of pearls and amber , by four Ivory
    steeds
Of perfect Christal ; this were worth
1920   presenting.
Or some bright cloud of Saphirs— — Fy
    you are all
So dull, you do not love me.
    Col. Y'are transported
1925 To strange impossibilities : our service
Shall wait upon your happiness.
    Qu. Nay, nay,
I know you laugh at me, and well you
    may ;
1930 I talk I know not what. I would 'twere
    fit
To ask one queston of ye.
    All. Madam, any thing.
    Qu. You'l swear that I am Idle, yet
1935   you know
'Tis not my custom ; Look upon me
    well ;
Am I as fair as *Herophil ?*
    Petr. Yes, Madam,
1940 Or any other creature else alive.
    Qu. You make me blush in troth.   O
        would the King
Could see me with your eyes.   Or
        would I were
1945 Much courser then I am to all the
    world ;
So I might onely seem more fair to him.
        Enter Velasco and Lodovico.

See here come more.   *Velasco,* thou art
    welcom.   1950
Welcom kinde *Lodovico.* You I know
Bring fresh supplies of comfort ; do not
    cloud
Your news with circumstance : Say, doth
    the King   1955
Expect me ? Yes, good man, I know he
    does.
Speak briefly, good my Lord, and truly.
    Velas. Madam, Take all at once, he is
        the King ;   1960
And Kings may do their pleasures.
    Qu. True, *Velasco.*
But I have from my heart forgot remem-
    brance
Of former passages, the world is chang'd. 1965
Is a' not justly royal ?
    Lodov. Would a' were , I wish it for
your sake Madam, but my wishes and his
inclinations are quite opposite.
    Petr. What said you, *Lodovico ?*   1970
    Lodov. Thus *Petruchi.* *Velasco* hath
been by the King disgrac'd, by his mini-
ons abused, baffled, they justified by the
King in't. In a word ; *Alphonso* is, and
will be the scourge of *Arragon.*   1975
    Qu. I'll stop my ears, they shannot let
    in poyson,
Rank treacherous searching poyson.
    Alm. 'Tis impossible.
    Qu. Yes, 'tis impossible ; but now I 1980
    see
Y'are all agreed to curse me in the hight
Of my prosperities. O that at once
I could have leave to dye and shun the
    times.   1985
        Enter Muretto.
    Muret. His excellent Majesty by me
commends to your Royal hands this let-
ter, Madam.
    Qu. Why thus I kiss,   1990
And kiss again ; Welcom, what e're it
    speaks.
    Muret. That you may all conceive
(my Lords) the Kings hearty zeal to u-
nity and goodness, he by me intreates 1995
your attendance on the Queen to him :
To you Signior, *Petruchi,* he sends this
Diamond from his own finger.
    Petr. You strike me into wonder.
    Muret. I should excuse his highness 2000
        violence

violence to you, my lord *Velasco*;
but he says, that your own indiscre-
tion deserv'd your late reproof : And
futher, (pardon me that I mince not
2005 the sum of his injunction) he says your
cowardice is now so vulgarly palpable,
that it cannot stand with his honour to
countenance so degenerating a spirit.

Velas. I thank him ; yet, if you re-
2010 member well ;
Both he and you prov'd me another
man.

Qu. The sweetest letter that ever was
writ :
2015 Come we must to the King——How !
'Tis my ring,
The first ring that I ever gave the King.
Petruchi, I must have it.

Petr. 'Twas the King sent it :
2020 *I* mean to yeeld it back again.

Qu. No I will.
And in exchange take that of equal
value ;
But not with me, 'cause it comes from
2025 my husband.
Let's slack no time, this day shall crown
our peace.

Exit all but Velasco and Lodovico.

Lodov. You see my Lord how the
2030 world goes.
What your next course ?

Velas. Would I could leave my self, I
am unfit
For company of men : Art thou my
2035 friend ?

Lodov. I cannot tell what I am, your
patient humor indeed perswades me I
am nothing.
Ladies little puppy dogs shortly will
2040 break your shins with milke-sops, and
you dare not cry, come out cur. Faith
tell me for our wonted frindships sake ;
hath not this Madam sweet heart of
yours a share in your Meramorphosis ?
2045 *Velas.* You are unkinde, as much as in
a thought,
To wrong her vertue. *Lodovico*, no ;
I have resolv'd never to fight again.

Lodov. 'Tis a very safe resolution : but
2050 have you resolv'd never to be beaten
again ?

Velas. That goodly sound of gallant
valiant man

Is but a breath, and dyes as soon as
utter'd.   2055
I'll seek my fame henceforward in the
praise
Of sufferance and patience, for rash
man-hood
Adds onely life to cruelty, yet by cru- 2060
elty
Takes life away, and leaves upon our
souls
Nothing but guilt, while patience if it
be   2065
Settl'd, doth even in bondage keep us
free.

Lodov. Excellent morality ; but good
my Lord, without more circumstance,
the cause, let me know the ground and 2070
cause on't.

Velas. My will, or if you please my
cowardice,
More ask not, more, I vow, you shall not
know.   2075

Enter Mopas.

Mop. O Fy, fy, I were better be the
Hangmans deputy, then my Lord *Velasco*'s Gentleman usher; all the streets as
I pass whoot at me, and ask me if I be so 2080
valiant as my master the coward ; they
swear their children carry woodden
daggers to play a prize with him, and
there's no talk but of the arrant coward
Velasco.   2085

Velas. I care not, let'em talk.

Mop. Care not ? By these hilts, I had
rather then a hundred ducates, I had
but as much spirit : as to have drawn
upon a couple of men in Ginger-bread, 2090
which a hucsters crook't legged whorson ape held up, and swore they were
two taller fellows then you are.

Lodov. Your readiest way were to
get you into a cloyster ; for there's no 2095
going to Court.

Mop: Yes, to have our brains rubb'd
out with the heel of a brown manchet.

Velas. As, y'are my friend forbear to 2100
come more neer me.   *Exit Velasco.*

Lodov. Gone so quickly ? *Mopas* I'll
finde out this mystery, and thou shalt be
the instrument.

Mop. Shall I ? Why agreed, let me 2105
alone

alone for an instrument, be it a winde or
string'd instrument , I'll sound at one
end or other I'll warrant ye.

Exeunt.

2110   *Enter Alphonso, Pynto, Bufo.*
        Alph. Are all things ready as we gave
charge?
        Pyn. Yes all, and the face of the hea-
vens are passing favourable.
2115   *Alph. Bufo,* Be it thy care, the watch
        word given,
To seize *Petruchi* suddenly.
        Buf. If the Devil be not in him, I'll
make him fast enough.
2120   *Alph.* Mean time wee'll take our
place, they are at hand.
Some sound our choisest musick t'entertain
This Queen with all the seeming forms
2125   of State.   *Loud Musick.*

        Enter Queen supported by Petruchi,
        Herophil, Collumello, Almada,
        and Muretto.

        All. All joy to *Aragons* great King.
2130   *Alph.* You strive to act in words (my
        lords) but we our self
Indeavor rather how to speak in act.
Now is a time of peace of amity.
The Queen is present ; Lady, seat you
2135   here,
As neer,as if we plac'd you in our heart,
Where you are deep inthron'd.
        Qu. As you in mine,
So may I ever live in yours, my Lord.
2140   *Alph.* How so? You are too charita-
        ble now,
That covet but equality in love ;
A cold,a frozen love ; for I must think
The streams of your affections are dry'd
2145   up ,
Or running from their wonted chan-
nels, range
In lawless paths of secresie and stealth ;
Which makes us love you more.
2150   *Qu.* I would your words
Dissented not from your resolved
thoughts
For then (if I mistake not) you would
feel

Extremity of passion, which indeed   2155
Is noble jealousie.
        Alph. Are you so plain ?
I thank you Madam ; lend me your fair
        hand,
What's here ? O my presages ! Whence   2160
        got you this ring ?
        Qu. This ring, my lord?
        Alph. This ring, my lord !
By honours reverend crest 'tis time to
        wake.   2165
Art thou not pale, *Petruchi ?*
        Petr. Gratious, Sir.
This is the ring you sent me by *Muretto,*
Which 'cause it came from you , the
        Queen would needs   2170
Exchange it for another of her own.
        Alph. True, 'cause it came from me, I
        take it so,
And grant ye, know the word. *'Tis won*
        and lost.   2175

        Enter a Guard, Bufo with them seize
        Petruchi ; Pynto the Queen.
        Petr. What mean ye, Helhounds ?
Slaves, let go my sword.
        Buf. Keep in your chaps, and leave   2180
scolding, my small friend, 'tis now no
time to wrangle or to rore.
        Qu. Nay, nay, with what you please I
am content.
        Col. What means your Highness?   2185
        Alm. wronge not Majesty
With such unnoble rigour.
        Alph. O, my lords,
The weight of all this shame falls hea-
        viest here   2190
In my afflicted bosome. Madman like
I would not credit, what mine ears had
        heard,
From time to time of that adulterous
        woman.   2195
For this have I liv'd widowed from her
        bed,
Was deaf to proofs, to oaths, and ever
        thought
That whoredom could not suit her self   2200
so trimly
On vertues outside. But *Petruchi* there
Hath a loud speaking conscience, can
        proclaim
Her lust, and my dishonour   2205
                    Petr. Grant

Petr. Grant me hearing.

Alph. Away with him to prison, make him fast

On pain of all your lives.

2210　*Buf.* Come, Sir, there is no playing fast and loose, which fit a ducat now.

Exit Bufo with Petruchi.

Col. But what now for the Queen?

Alph. As she deserves.

2215　*Alm.* Our law requires a clear and open proof,

And a juditial trial.

Alph. Yes to subjects

It does, but who among you dares speak

2220　justice

Against your natural Soveraign? Not one.

Pyn. Your Majesty hath most wisely considered that point.

2225　*Muret.* I have stood silent all this while, and cannot but with astonishment and unutterable grief bear a share of sadness in these disasters. But, Madam, be not altogether dejected on your part:

2230　there is more mercy in this sovraign Prince, then that you should any way distrust.

Qu. Nay, even proceed and question me no more.

2235　*Alph.* I will be gentle to you, and the course

That I will take shall merit your best thanks.

If in a moneth a Champion shall appear,

2240　In single opposition to maintain

Your honor; I will be the man my self

In person to avouch this accusation:

And which of us prevails, shall end this strife.

2245 But if none come, then you shall lose your head.

Mean time your usage shall be like a Queen.

Muret. Now by the life of honour, 'tis

2250 a most Princely tryal, and will be worth you eternal memory.

Qu. Where must I then be led!

Alph. No where but here

In our own palace; and as I am King,

2255 None worse then I shall be her Guardian.

Alm. Madam, Heaven is the Guardian of the just;

You cannot miss a Champion.

Qu. E're I go,　　　　　2260

May I entreat a word?

Alph. O yes, you may.

Qu. Collumello and *Almado,* hear me,

I speak to you, and to your felow Peers,

Remember both by oaths and by alle- 2265

giance

You are my subjects.

Both. Madam, true, we are.

Qu. Then as you ever bore respect or truth　　　　　2270

To me as to your Soveraign, *I* conjure ye

Never to levy arms against the King,

Singly or openly, and never else

To justifie my right or wronge in this.

For if you do, here *I* proclaim ye all　　2275

Traytors to loyalty and me: for surety,

I crave your oaths a new.

Both. Since you enforce us,

We sware: and heaven protect you.

Qu. Let me be gone.　　　　　2280

Alph. Well as they please for that:

Muretto, follow.

Exit all but Almada and Collummello.

Alm. Here is fine work, my lord.

What's to be done?　　　　　2285

Col. Stand still while this proud Tyrant cuts our throats.

Alm. She's wrong'd, and this is onely but a plot.

Velasco, now might binde his Country to 2290

him;

But he is grown so cowardly and base,

That boys and children beat him as they list.

Col. I have be thought me, we, with 2295

th' other Peers,

Will set a proclamation out, assuring

What worthy Knight soever undertakes,

By such a day, as Champion for the Queen.　　　　　2300

Shall have a hundred thousand ducats paid,

Withal, what honors else he shall demand.

Alm. This must be speeded, or 'twill 2305

come to late.

Col. It shall be suddain: Here our hope must stand;

Kings command Subjects; Heav'n doth

Kings command.　　　　　*Exeunt.* 2310

Act IV.

Act IV.

Enter Salassa and Shaparoon.

Salas. A coward ? 'tis impossible ; *Velasco* a coward ? The brave man ? The
2315 wonder of the time ? Sure , *Shaparoon*, 'tis a meer scandal rais'd by an
enemy.

Shap. 'Tis most certain, most apparent ; Taylors, Prentizes, nay, Bakers
2320 and Weavers ; (things that drink cannot put spirit into, they are such mighty
bread-eaters) they as I am an honest woman, fling old shoes at him, and he
dares not turn back to give an angry
2325 word.

Salas. I had been sweetly promoted to such a tame Champion.

Shap. Gallants *!* Out upon 'em, 'tis your tough clown is your only raiser up
2330 of man or woman.

Salas. A Proclimation is sent out for certain *?*

Shap. Most assuredly.

Salas. The sum proposed, a hundred
2335 thousand ducats.

Shap. Present payment, without attendance.

Salas. 'Tis a glorious reward — — speak low, and observe.

2340   *Enter Mopas reading a Proclamation.*

Mop. Whosoever, man or woman, can, or will procure any such foresaid defendant, against the said day ; let them, him, or she repair to the said lords of the
2345 Councel , and give in such sufficient assurance for such defence, and they or
any of them shall receive a hundred thousand ducats in ready cash ; with
what honors may give them, him, or
2350 her content or satisfaction.

O that I durst be valiant : A hundred thousand. A hundred thousand ; how
it rumbles in my chops.

Salas. Prethee, a word, my friend.
2355   *Mop.* Sweet Lady, all fair weather upon ye.

As for you, Madam, time was, I recommend to your ancient remembrance ,
time is past : with my service forwards and backwards, when 'tis time present, 2360
resting yours in the whole *Mopas.*

Shap. Very courtly and pithy.

Salas. Pray let me view your paper.

Mop 'Tis your ladiships.

Shap. Some proclamation as I take it. 2365

Mop. Madam Reverence, you have taken it in the right cue.

Salas. I am o'rejoy'd ; there's gold for thy news. Friend. I will make thee the
happiest and most welcom messenger to 2370 thy lord , that ever received thanks
from him ; without delay, wait on me for instructions.

Mop. I am at your ladiships beck.

                              Exeunt. 2375
    Enter Alphonso, and Muretto.

Muret. True, true, Sir, you are set high upon the stage for action. O the top of
my ambition, my hearts Idol *!*
What a perplexity are you twin'd into? 2380
And justly ; so justly , that it is hard to judge, whether your happiness were
greater in the possession of an unmatchable beauty, or your prefent misery, by
inforcing that beauty to expose her ho- 2385 nor to so apparent a contempt : This is
not the least, that might have been in time prevented.

Alph. O I am lost *Muretto*, my sunke
    eyes   2390
Are buried in their hollows : busie
    thoughts
Press on like legions of infernal hags
To menace my destruction : Yet my
    judgment   2395
Still prompts my senses, that my Queen
    is fair.

Muret. Fair ! Uuspeakable workmanship of Heavens bounty. Were all the
skilfullest Painters that ever discern'd 2400 colours, moulded into one, to perfect an
Artist.   Yet that Artist should sooner want fansie or imagination , for perso-
nating a curious medal , then ever to patern a counterfeit so exquisitely ex- 2405
cellent, as is the Queen by nature.

Alph. I have surveyed the wonder of
    her cheeks,
Compar'd them wth the lillies and the
    rose   And 2410

And by my life, *Muretto*, Roses are
Adulterate to her blush, and lilies pale,
Examin'd with her white ; yet, blear
   eyed fool,
2415 I could not see those rarities before
   me.
   Muret. Every man is blind (my lord)
in his own happiness, there's the curse
of our mortality.
2420 She was the very tale of the world :
Her perfections busied all tongues.
She was the onely wish of *Europes* chief-
   est Monarchs.
Whose full fruition you (and 'twas your
2425 capital sin) most inhumanly abandoned.
   Alph. Villain, *Petruchi*, let me for ever
curse him : Had he not been the man ;
who else had durst to hazard a denyal
from her scorns ?
2430 *Muret.* See now herein you are monstrous discourteous, above excuse ; why,
Sir, what hath *Petruchi* done ? Which
(from any King to a Vassal) al men would
not eagerly have persued. Alas, my lord,
2435 his nobleness is eternal, by this means, in
attempting and his felicity unmatchable,
in injoying the glory of his time, a beau
so conquering, so unparalell'd.
   Alph. She is superlative.
2440 *Muret.* Divine.
   Alph. Rich, bright.
   Muret. immortal.
   Alph. Too too worthy for a man.
   Mur. The Gods might enjoy her.
2445 *Alph.* Nature ne're fram'd so sweet a
creature.
   Muret. She is self Nature's Nature.
   Alph. Let me for ever curse the frail
   condition
2450 Of our deluded faculties : *Muretto*,
Yet being all, as she is all, her best
Is worst considering that she is a wanton
   Muret. Build you a Palace, arch it
2455 with Diamonds, roof it with Carbun-
cles, pave it with Emraulds, daub it
with Gold, furnish it with all what cost
can lay on, and then seal up the doors,
and at best 'tis but a solitary nest for
2460 Owles and *Daws.*
Beauty was not meerly created for wonder, but for use : 'Tis you were in the

fault ; 'tis you perswaded her, urg'd,
compell'd, inforc'd her : I know it, my
truth and plainness trumpets it out to 2465
ye *:* Besides, women (my lord) are all
creatures, not Gods nor Angels.
   Alph. I must confess 'tis true, yet by
   my Crown
She dyes, if none defend her, I'm re- 2470
   solv'd.
   Muret. 'Tis a heroical disposition, and
with your honour she cannot, must not
live. Here's the point ; If she live and you
receive her to favour, you will be a no- 2475
ted Cuckold ; which is a recognizance
dishonorable to all, but to a King fearfully infamous. On the other side, if you
prevail, and she be put to death, you do
as it were deprive the Firmament of the 2480
Sun, and your self of the treasure of the
whole earth.
   Alph. Right, right; *Muretto*, there thou
   strik'st the wound
Too deeply to be cur'd, yet I must do't. 2485
I would fain see her now.
   Muret. Pray do, Sir ; and let *Petruchi*
come face to face to her ; observe them
both, but be very mild to both *:* use extremity to neither. 2490
   Alph. Well counsell'd ; call them hither, but none with them :
Wee'll strive with grief ; Heaven ! I am
   plung'd at full.
Never henceforward shall I slumber out 2495
One peaceful hour ; my enraged blood
Turns coward to mine houour. I could
   wish
My Queen might live now though I did
   but look 2500
And gaze upon her cheeks, her ravishing
   cheeks.
But, oh, to be a Cuckold ; 's death, she
   dyes.

Enter at one door Petruchi, and the 2505
   other Muretto and the Queen, they
   stand at several ends of the
   Stage.
   Muret. My gratious Lord.
   Alph. Reach yond fair sight a chair, 2510
That man a stool, sit both, wee'll have
   it so.
   Mur. 'Tis Kingly done ; in any case
         E   (my

my lord curb now a while the vio-
2515 lence of your passion, and be tempe-
rate.

   Qu. Sir, 'tis my part to kneel, for on
your brow
I read sad sentence of a troubled wrath,
2520 And that is argument enough to prove
my guilt, not being worthy of your favour.

   Petr. Let me kneel too, though not
for pardon. yet
2525 In duty to this presence : else I stand
As far from falsehood, as is that from
truth

   Muret. Nay, Madam, this not the promise on your part.
2530 It is his pleasure you should sit.

   Qu. His pleasure is my law.

   Alph. Let him sit too,the man,   }Both
   Petr. Sir, you are obey'd.   }sit.

   Alph. Between my comforts and my
2535   shame I stand
In equal distance ; this way let me turn
To thee thou woman. Let me dull mine
eyes
With surfeit on thy beauty. What art
2540   thou
Great dazeling splendor ? Let me ever
look
And dwell upon this presence.

   Muret. Now it works.
2545   *Alph.* I am distract. Say ? What !
Do not, do not——

   Muret. My lord the King—Why, Sir ?—
He is in a trance, or else metamorphis'd
to some some pillar of marble : How fix-
2550 edly a' stands.
D'ee hear, Sir ? What d'ee dream on ?
My lord, this is your Queen speak to
her.

   Alph. May I presume with my irreve-
2555   rent lips
To touch your sacred hand.

   Qu. I am too wretched
To be thought but the subject of your
mirth.
2560   *Alph.* Why she can speak, *Muretto* ? O
tell me pray,
And make me ever, ever fortunate ;
Are you a mortal creature ? Are ye indeed
2565 Moulded of flesh and blood like other
women ?

Can you be pittiful ? Can ye vouchsafe
To entertain fair parley ? Can you love,
Or grant me leave to love you; can you,
  say ?   2570

   Qu. You know too well, my lord, in-
stead of granting,
I ow a duty, and must sue to you,
If I may not displease.

   Alph. Now I am great,   2575
You are my Queen, and I have wrong'd
  a merit,
More then my service in the humblest
lowness
Can ever recompence. I'll rather wish 2580
To meet whole hosts of dangers, and en-
counter
The flabled whips of steel, then ever
part
From those sweet eyes : not time shall 2585
sue divorce
'Twixt me and this great miracle of Na-
ture.

  Muretto ?

   Muret. Soveraign Sir.   2590

   Alph. I'll turn away,
And mourn my former errors——Worse
then death
Look where a Basilisk with murthering
  flames   2595
Of poyson, strikes me Blinde. Insatiate
tempter,
Patern of lust, 'tis thou alone hast sun-
dred
Our lawful bride bed, planted on my 2600
crest
The horned Satyrs badge ; hast soyl'd a
beauty
As glorious,as sits yonder on her front.
Kill him, *Muretto*, why should he re- 2605
ceive
The benefit of the law, that us'd no
law
In my dishonours ?

   Petr. Were you more a King   2610
Then Royalty can make you , though
opprest
By your commanding powers, yea, and
curb'd
In bonds most falsely, yet, give me a 2615
sword
And strip me to my shirt,I will defend
Her spotless vertue, and no more esteem,
                         In

In such a noble cause, an host of Kings,
2620 Then a poor stingless swarm of buzzing
　　flies.
　　　*Qu. Petruchi,*in those words thou dost
　　　condemn
　　Thy loyalty to me, I shall disclaim
2625 All good opinion of thy worth or truth,
　　If thou persevere *to* affront my lord.
　　　Petr. Then I have done. Here's mise-
　　　ry unspeakable ;
　　Rather to yeeld me guilty wrongfully,
2630 Then contradict my wrongs.
　　　Alph. High impudence.
　　Could she be ten times fairer then she is,
　　Yet I would be reveng'd.　You sweet,
　　　I would
2635 Again——Her beams quite blast me.
　　　Muret. If you will be an Eaglet of the
　　right aery, you must endure the Sun.
　　Can you chuse but love her ?
　　　*Alph.*No by the Stars. Why would not
2640 you be honest;and know how I do dote?
　　　Qu. May I be bold
　　To say I am, and not offend ?
　　　Alph. Yes, yes,
　　Say so for heavens love, though you be
2645　as fowl
　　As sin can black your purity.　Yet tell
　　　me　　　·
　　That are white and chast ; That
　　　while you live
2650 The span of your few dayes, I may re-
　　　joyce
　　In my deluded follies'; least I dye
　　Through anguish, e're I have reveng'd
　　　my injury,
2655 And so leave you behind me for another;
　　That were intollerable.
　　　Qu. Heaven knows, I ne're abus'd my
　　self or you.
　　　Petr. As much sware I,and truly.
2660　*Alph.* Thou proud Devil,
　　Thou hast a lying tongue; They are con-
　　sented
　　In mischief.　Get ye hence seducing
　　horrors.
2665 I'll stop mine eyes and ears till you are
　　gone,
　　As you would be more merciful, away,
　　Or as you would finde mercy.
　　　　Ex. Queen Petruchi contrary waies.
2670　Muret. Sir, they are gone.

　　Alph. And she too then let me be seen
　　no more.
I am distracted, both waies I feel my
　　blame ;
To leave her death, to live with her is 2675
　　shame.　　　　　　*Exit.*
　Muret. Fare ye well King, this is ad-
mirable , I will be chronicled, all my
business ripens to my wishes.　And if
honest intentions thrive so succesfully ; 2680
I will henceforth build upon this assurance, that there can hardly be a greater
Hell or Damnation, then in being a Vil-
lane upon earth.　　　　*Exit.*

　Enter Lodovico, Salassa, Shaparoon.　2685

　Lodov. I am wonder stricken --And
were you i'faith the she indeed , that
turn'd my Lords heart so handsomly, so
cunningly?O how I reverence wit. Well,
lady, you are as pestilent a piece of po- 2690
licy, as ever made an ass of love.
　Salas. But, *Lodovico,* I'll salve all a-
gain quickly.
　Shap. Yes indeed forsooth, she has the
trick on't.　　　　　　　2695
　Lodov. You have undertaken with the
lords already, you say.
　Salas. I have, and my life is at stake,
but I fear not that.
　Lodov. Pish, you have no need ; one 2700
smile,or kinde simper from you does all;
I warrant ye the sight of so much gold,
as you are to receive , hath quickned
your love infinitely.
　Salas. Why, Sir, I was not worthy 2705
of my lords love before ;　I was too
poor : but now two hundred thousand
ducats, is a dower fit for a lord.
　Lodov. Marry is't.　I applaud your
　consideration.　　　　　2710
'Twas neatly thought on.

　Enter Collumello and Almada.

　Col. Have you prevail'd yet, lady,time
　runs on,
You must not dally.　　　　2715
　Salas. Good my lords, fear nothing :
Were it but two hours to't, I should be
　ready.
　　　　　　　E 2　　　　*Enter*

Enter Velasco very sad.

2720 *Lodov.* He comes himself, 'tis fit we stood unseen.

Ply him soundly, lady.

Alm. Let us withdraw then.   *Exeunt.*

Velas. I cannot be alone, still I am

2725 hunted

With my confounding thoughts : Too late I finde,

How passions at their best are but sly traytors

2730 To ruin honour. That which we call love,

Was by the wisest power above fore-thought

To check our pride. Thus when men are

2735 blown up

At the highest of conceit, then they fall down

Even by the peevish follies of their frailties.

2740 *Salas.* The best of my Lord *Velasco's* wishes ever.

Crown him with all true content.

Velas. Cry ye mercy, Lady.

Salas. I come to chide you my Lord ;

2745 can it be possible that ever any man could so sincerely profess such a migh-tiness of affection, as you have done to me , and forget it all so soon, and so un-kindely.

2750 *Velas.* Are you a true very lover, or are you bound

For pennance to walk to some holy shrine

In visitation ? I have seen that face.

2755 *Salas.* Have you so ? O you are a hot lover ; a woman is in fine case to weep out her eyes for so uncertain a friend, as your protestations urg'd me to conceive you : But come I know what you'll say

2760 aforehand, *I* know you are angry.

Velas. Pray give me leave to be my own tormentor.

Salas. Very angry, extreamly angry ; But as *I* respect perfection, tis more then

2765 *I* deserve.

Little know you the misery *I* have en-dured, and all about a hasty word of nothing, and *I'*ll have it prove nothing e're we part.

2770 *Velas.* Her pride hath made her luna-tick, alas !

She hath quite lost her wi ts, those are the fruits

Of scorns and mockeries.

Salas. To witness how indearedly I 2775 prefer your merits, and love your per-son ; in a word, my lord, I absolve you, and set you free from the injunction I bound you in ; as I desire to thrive, I meant all but for a tryal in jest.   2780

Velas. these are no words of madness; whither tends

The extremity of your invention , Lady ?

I'll swear no more.   2785

Salas. I was too blame, but one fault (me thinks) is to be pardoned, when I am yours and you firmly mine : I'll bear with many in you.

Velas. So, if you be in earnest ; What's 2790 the matter ?

Salas. The sum of all is, that *I* know it suits not with the bravery of the lord *Velasco's* spirit, to suffer his Queen and soveraign stand wrongfully accused 2795 of dishonour, and dye shamefully for a fault never committed.

Velas. Why 'tis no fault of mine.

Salas. Nor shall it be of mine : Go be a famous subject ; be a ransomer of thy 2800 Queen from dangers , be registred thy Countries patron : Fight in defence of the fairest and innocentest princess a-live : *I* with my heart release you.

First conquer ; that done, enjoy me 2805 ever for thy wife : *Velasco, I* am thine.

Velas. Pish, you release me, all their cunning strains

Of policy that set you now a work,

To treble ruin me, in life, fame, soul, 2810

Are foolish and unable to draw down

A greater wrath upon my head ; in troth

You take a wrong course lady.

Salas. Very good, Sir, 'tis prettily put 2815 off, and wondrous modestly.   I protest no man hath enjoyn'd me to this task ; 'tis onely to do service to the State, and honour to you.

Velas. No man enjoyn'd you but your 2820 self ?

Salas. None else, as *I* ever had truth in me.

                              Velas. Know

Velas. Know then from me, you are a
2825   wicked woman,
And avarice, not love to me, hath forc'd
  ye
To practice on my weakness. *I* could
  raile ,
2830 Be most uncivil ; But take all in short:
I know you not.
  Salas. Better and better , the man
will triumph anon sure ; Prethee, good
dissemble no longer ; I say you shall
2835 fight, *I'll* have it so : *I* command you
fight, by this kiss you shall.
  Velas. Forbear, let me in peace bid
you forbear ;
I will be henceforth still a stranger to
2840   you,
Ever a stranger, look, look up, up there
My oath is bookt , no humane power
  can free me.
  Salas. I grant you none but *I.*
2845   *Velas.* Be not deceived, *I* have
Forgot your scorns; you are lost to me,
Witness the Genius of this place, how
  e're
You tempt my constancy, *I* dare not
2850   fight.
  Salas. Not dare to fight, what not for
me *?*
  Velas. No Lady.
I durst not, must not, cannot, will not
2855   fight.
  Salas. O me undone.
  Velas. What ayles you ?
  Salas. Now my life
Hath run it's last for I have pawn'd it Sir
2860 To bring you forth as champion for the
  Queen.
  Velas. And so should have the pro-
mis'd Gold.
  Salas. I, I.
2865   *Velas.* You have reveng'd my wrongs
  upon your selfe.
I cannot helpe you, nay alas you know
  It lay not in me.
  Salas. O take pitty on mee,
2870 Look heer, I hold my hands up, bend
  my knees,
Heaven can require no more.
  Velas. Then kneel to heaven
I am no God, I cannot do you good.
2875   *Salas.* Shall not my tears prevayle *?*

hard-hearted Man.
Dissembler, loves dishonour, bloody but-
  cher
Of a poor Lady, be assured my Ghost
Shall haunt thy soule when I am dead. 2880
  Velas. Your curse
Is falne upon youur own head , herein
  show
A noble piety, to beare your death
With resolution, and for finall answer 2885
Lady I will not fight to gain the world.
                  Exit.
  Salas. Gone ! I have found at length
  my just reward ,
And henceforth must prepare to welcom 2890
  Death.
Velasco I begin to love thee now.
Now I perceave thou art a noble man,
Compos'd of Goodnes, what a foole was I?
It grieves me more to loose him then to 2895
  die.
  Enter Almada , Columello , Lodovico ,
      Shaproon.
  Coll. Lady we have heard all that now
  hath past,   2900
You have deceav'd your selfe and us ,
  the time
We should have spent in seeking other
  means.
Is lost, of which you are the cause.   2905
  Alm. And for it
The senats strickt decree craves execu-
  tion,
what can you say ?
  Salas. My Lords I can no more   2910
but yeild me to the law.
  Shap. O that ever you were born, you
have made a sweet hand on't, have you
not.
  Lodov. Here is the right recompence 2915
of a vain confidence, Mistresse : But I
will not torture you being so neer your
end, lady say your prayers and die in
Charity, that's all the pitty I can take
on ye   *Exit Lodovico.* 2920
  Coll. Ten times the gold you should
have had, now Lady cannot release you.
  Alm. You alone are shee
Ruins your country. Heres the price
  of sin,   2925
Ill thrift, all loose in seeking all to win.
         Exit. all but shaproon.
           Shap. Nay

Shap. Nay even go thy ways, 'tis an old proverbe that leachery and cove-
2930 tousnes go together, and 'tis a true one too, But I'le shift for one.

If some proper squire or lustly yeoman have a mind to any thing I have about me, 'a shall soon know what to trust too
2935 for I see the times are very troublesome.

Enter Pynto.

Pyn. Now is the prosperous season when the whole round of the planets are coupling together.   Let birds and
2940 beasts observe valentines day, I am a man and all times are with me in season, this same Court ease hath sett my blood on tiptoe, I am Madder then a march hare.

2945 *Shap.* Blessing on your fair face, your handsome hand, your clean foot sir, are you a Courtier sir?

Pyn. Good starrs direct me, sweet wo-man, I am a Courtier, if you have any
2950 suit, what is't, what is't? be short.

Shap. Lord what a Courteous proper man 'a is, trust me, 'a hath a most elo-quent beard. --- Suit Sir, Yes Sir, I am a countrey gentlewoman by father and
2955 Mothers side, one that comes to see fa-shions and learne newes.   And How I pray sir (if I may be so bold to aske) stand things at Court Sir now a dayes?

Pyn. A very modest necessary and dis-
2960 creet Qeustion.

Indeed Mistris Countrey-Gentlewoman, things at Court stand as they were ever wont, some stiffe and some slacke, every thing according to the imployment it
2965 hath.

Shap. Mary, the more pitty sir, that they have not all good doing a like, me-thinkes, they should be all and at all times ready heer.

2970 *Pyn.* You speake by a figure, by your leave, in that.

But because you are a stranger, I will a litte more amply informe you.

Heer at our Court of *Arragon,* Schollars
2975 for the most part are the veriest fooles for that they are allways beggerly and prowd.   And foolish citizens the wisest schollars for that they never run at char-ges for greater learning to cast up their

reck'nings, then their Horn-book.   2980
Here every old lady is cheaper then a proctor, and will as finely convey an o-pen act, without any danger of a con-sistory. Love and money sweepes all be-fore them, be they cut or longtayle. Do 2985
not I deserve a kisse for this discovery Mistris.

Shap. A kisse, O my dear chastity, yes indeed forsooth, and I pray please your selfe.   2990

Pyn. Good wench by venus, but are you any thing rich?

Shap. Rich enough to serve my turn.

Pyn. I see you are reasonable fair.

Shap. I ever thought my selfe so.   2995

Pyn. Will you survey my lodgings?

Shap. At your pleasure sir being un-der your gard as *I* am.

Enter Mopas and Bufo.

Buf. Sirrha *Mopas,* If my mistresse say 3000
but the word, thou shalt see what an ex-ployt, I will doe.

Mop. You'le undertake it you say, though your throat be cut in your own defence, 'tis but manslaughter, you can 3005
never be hang'd for it.

Buf. Nay I am resolute in that point, heer's my hand, let him shrinke, that list, I'le not flinch a hayres breadth *Mopas.*   3010

Mop. What, old huddle and twang so close at it, and the dog dayes so neer, Heark ye, your lady is going the way of all flesh. And so is that scholler with you methinkes, though not in the same cue, 3015
is 'a not?

Shap. 'A has promist to tell me my fortune at his chamber, and do me some other good for my ladies safety.

Pyn. I have spoken, the planets shall 3020
be rul'd by me, Captain, you know they shall.

Buf. Let the planets hang themselves in the elements, what care I, I have o-ther matters to trouble my braines.   3025

Mop. Signior *Pynto* take her to you, as true a mettall'd blade as ever was turn'd into a dudgion, hearke in your eare.

Enter Lodovico and Herophill.

Lodov. I know not how to trust you, 3030
you ar all so fickle so unconstant.

Her. If

Herop. If I faile
Let me be mark't a Strumpet.

Lodov. I apprehend you use him kind-
3035 ly still,
See where 'a is , Captain you are well
mett,
Her'es one whose heart you have.

Herop. He knowes he has.

3040 *Buf.* Why by my troth I thanke you
forsooth, 'tis more of your curtesie then
my deserving, but I shall study to deserve
it.

Herop. I hope so, and doubt it not.

3045 *Lodov.* Madam Cosen *Shaproon.*

Shap. You are welcom sir.

Pyn. Cosen, Nay then I smell she is a
gentlewoman indeed.

Mop. Yes, and as antiently descended
3050 as Flesh and blood can derive her.

Pyn. I am a made man and I will have
her.

Herop. You'le walke with me sir ?

Buf. Even through fire and water.
3055 sweet Mistres.

Lodov. Let's every one to what con-
cerns us most,
For now's the time all must be sav'd or
lost.   *Exeunt all.*

3060   **Act V.**

A Scassold

Enter Velasco and Lodovico.

Velas. This is not kindly done , nor
like a friend.

3065 *Lodov.* Keep your chamber then, what
should owles and batts do abroad by day
light ? why, you are become so notori-
ously ridiculous, that a Craven is repu-
ted of nobler spirit amongst birds, then
3070 *Velasco* among men.

Velas. Why *Lodovico* dost thou tempt
my wrongs ?
O friend, 'tis not an honor or a fame
Can be a gain to me , though I should
3075 dare
To entertain this Combatt, say my fate

Did crown mine arm with conquest of
the King,
Put case the cause add glory to the jus-
tice   3080
Of my prevaling sword ? what can I win?
Saving a pair of lives I lose a soule ,
My rich soule *Lodovico,* Does not yet
The heart even shrill within thee ? All
thy spirits   3085
Melt into Passions, All thy manhood
stagger
Like mine ? Nay canst thou chuse but
now confess
That this word Coward is a name of 3090
Dignity ?

Lodov. Faint hearts and strong toungs
are the tokens of many a tall prattling
Ghossipe. Yet the truth is you have halfe
convinced me, But to what end will you 3095
be a looker on the Tragedy of this shee
Beast ? it will but breed your greater
vexation.

Velas. I hope not so, I looke for Comfort in't.   3100

Lodov. Mass : that may be too, It cannot but make your melancholy a little
merry, to see the woodcockes neck
caught in a worse noose, then shee had
set for you.   3105

Velas. That's but a poor revenge, I'de
rather weep
On her behalfe, but that I hope her courage
Will triumph over Death.   3110

Lodov. My Lord they come.

Velas. Let me stand back unseen, Good
Angells guard her.

Velasco Muffles himselfe.

Enter executioner before Salassa. her 3115
Hayre loose, after her , Almada,
Collumello and officers.

Alm. Tis a sad welcom.
To bid you welcome to the stroak of
Death.   3120
Yet you are come too't Lady.

Coll. And a curse
Throughout the land will be your ge-
nerall knell,
For having bin the wilfull overthrow, 3125
First of your Countreys Champion, next
your Queen ,
                                    Your

Your Lawfull Soveraign, who this very day.

3130 Must act a part which you must act before,

but with less guilt.

Alm. Use no long speeches lady,

The danger of the time, calls us away,

3135 We cannot listen to your farewells now.

Sal. I have few words to say, my heart is lodg'd

In yon same upper Parliament, yet now

If ere I part, and shall be seen no more,

3140 Some man of mercy could but truly speake

One word of pardon from the Lord Velasco,

My peace were made in earth, and I

3145 should fly

With wings of speed to Heaven.

Alm. Pish here's not any.

Salas. Not any? on then, why should I prolong

3150 A minute more of life, that live so late,

Where most I strive for love to purchace hate,

Beare witnes Lords I wish not to call back

3155 My younger dayes in promise that I would

Redeem my fault and do *Velasco* right,

But could I but reverse the doom of time,

3160 I would with humblest suit make prayers to heaven

For his long florishing welfare.

Col. Dispatch, dispatch;

You should have thought on this before,

3165 pray now

For your own health, for you have need to pray.

Lodov. Madam *Salassa*, I am bold to take leave of ye before your long journey: All

3170 the comfort that I can give you is, that the weather is like to hold very fair, you need not take much care for either hood or cloke for the matter.

Salas. Are you come? Worthy Sir,

3175 then I may hope

Your noble friend hath sent one gentle sigh

To grace my funeral : For vertues sake

Give me a life in death ; tell me, O tell

3180 me,

If he but seal my pardon, all is well.

Lodov. Say ye so? Why then in a word, go merrily up the stayers ; my lord *Velasco* desires Heaven may as heartily forgive him, as he does you.   3185

Salas. Enough, I thank his bounty, on I go   *goes up the Scaffold.*

To smile on horror : so, so, I'm up.

Great in my lowness, and to witness further   3190

My humbleness, here let me kneel and breath

My penitence : O women in my fall,

Remember that your beauties, youth and pride   3195

Are but gay tempters, 'less you wisely shun

The errors of your frailties : let me ever

Be an example to all fickle dames,

That folly is no shrine for vertuous 3200 names.

Heaven pardon all my vanities, and free

The lord *Velasco*, what e're come of me.

Bless, bless, the lord *Velasco.*--Strike.

As he is about to strike, Velasco *steps out.* 3205

Velas. Villain, hold, hold! Or thou dyest, Slave.

Alm. What means that countermand?

Lodov. Hey, do! More news yet, you 3210 will not be valiant when 'tis too late, I trust?

Velas. Woman, come down : Who lends me now a sword?

Lodov. Marry, that do I, Sir, I am your 3215 first man ; Here, here, here, take heed you do not hurt your fingers ; 'twill cut plaguely : and what will you do with it?

Velas. Base woman, take thy life, thy 3220 cursed life,

I set thee free, and for it pawn a soul :

But that I know heaven hath more store of mercy,

Then thou and all thy sex of sin and 3225 falsehood.

My Lords, I now stand Champion for the Queen :

Doth that discharge her?

Col. Bravest man, it doth :   3230

Lady, y'are safe ; now, Officers away.

This is a blessed hour !   *Ex. Officers.*

Alm. You

Alm. You shall for ever
Bind us your servants.

3235   *Lodov.* Aha : Why then, however
things happen, let them fall, as they fall.
God a' mercy, my lord, at last.

    Col. Hark how the people ring apeal
of joy,   *Shout within.*

3240 For this good news. My lord, time steals
away ;
We may not linger now.

    Salas. You give me life ;
Take it not, Sir, away again. I see

3245 Upon your troubled eyes such discontent
As frights my trembling heart ; Dear
Sir——

Velas. The Gold

3250 You hazarded your life for, is your own,
You may receive it at your pleasure.

    Alm. Yes,
'Tis ready for you, lady.

    Salas. Gold ? Let gold,

3255 And all the treasures of the earth besides
Perish like trash ; I value nothing, Sir,
But your assured love.

    Velas. My love ! Vain woman,
Henceforth thus turn I from thee, never

3260   look
For Apish dotage, for a smile, a how d'ee,
A fare ye well, a thought from me: let
Snakes
Live in my bosom, and with muderous

3265   stinges
Infect the vital warmth, that lends them
life,
If ever I remember thee or thine.
If I prevail, my services shall crave

3270 But one reward, which shall be, if that
ever
Thou come but in my sight, the State wil
please
To banish thee the land ; or else I vow,

3275 My self to leave it.

    Salas. My ill purchast life !

    Velas. Ill purchast life, indeed, whose
ransom craves
A sadder price, then price of bloodshed

3280   saves.
Go, learn bad woman, what it is, how
foul,
By gaining of a life, to lose a soul.
The price of one oul doth exceed as far

A life here, as the Sun in light a Star. 3285
Here though we live some threescore
years, or more,
Yet we must dye at last , and quit the
score
We ow to nature. But the soul once 3290
dying,
Dyes ever, ever ; no repurifying ;
No earnest sighs or grones ; no intercession ;
No tears; no pennance ; no too late con- 3295
fession
Can move the ear of justice, if it doom
A soul past cure to an infernal tomb.
Make use of this *Salassa.*

    Lodov. Think upon that now, and 3300
take heed, you look
My lord no more in the face.

    Salas. Goodness protect him! now my
life so late
I strove to save, which being sav'd I 3305
hate.   *Exeunt all.*

  Enter Alphonso armed all save the head,
    leading the Queen, a Herauld going
      before, Muretto , Herophil,
        a Guard.   3310

    Alph. Are you resolv'd to dye ?

    Qu. When life is irksom
Death is a happiness.

    Alph. Yes, if the cause
Make it not infamous : But when a 3315
beauty
So most incomparable as yours, is blemish'd
With the dishonorable stamp of whoredom :   3320
When your black tainted name, which
should have been
(Had you preserv'd it nobly) your best
Chronicle,
Wherein you might have liv'd , when 3325
this is stain'd,
And justly too ; then death doth but
heap
Affliction on the dying. Yet you see
With what a sympathie of equal grief 3330
I mourn your ruine.

    Qu. Would you could as clearly
Perceive mine innocence, as I can clearly
Protest it.   F   *Alph.* Fy,

3335 *Alph.* Fy to justify a sin
Is worse then to commit it, now y'are
    faulty.
    Muret. What a royall pair of excel-
lent creatures are heer both upon the
3340 castaway. It were a saint like mercy in
you (my Lord) to remitt the memory of
a past errour . And in you Madam (if
you be guilty of the supposed crime) to
submitt your selfe to the King.   I dare
3345 promise, his love to you is so unfayned,
that it will relent in your humility. Pray
do, good Madam do.
    Qu. But how if I be free ?
    Muret. By any means, for your honors
3350 cause do not yeeld then one jot.   Let
not the faint feare of Death deject you
before the royalty of an erected heart.
D'ee heare this my Lord, 'tis a doubtfull
case, almost impossible to be decided ,
3355 Look upon her well, as I hope to pros-
per, shee hath a most vertuous, a most innocent countenance.   Never heed it. I
know my Lord your jealousy and your
affectionswrestle together within you for
3360 them astery. Mark her beauty throughly.
Now by all the power of Love, tis pitty
Shee should not be as fair within as
    without.
    Alph. Could that be prov'd, *I'de* give
3365   my kingdom straight
And live a slave to her, and her perfecti-
    ons.
    Enter Almada, Columello, Attendants.
Lords welcome, see thus arm in arm we
3370   pace
To the wide theater of blood and shame
My Queen and *I,* my Queen ? had shee
    bin still
As shee was, mine, we might have liv'd
3375   too happ'ly,
For eithers comfort. Heer on this sweet
    modell,
This plott of wonder, this fair face, stands
    fixt
3380 My whole felicity on earth.   *In* witnes
Whereof, behold (my Lords) those
    manly tears
Which her unkindnes and my cruell fate
Force from their quiet springs , They
3385   speak alowd
To all this open ayre, their publick eyes,

That whither *I* kill or dy in this attempt
I shall in both be vanquisht.
    Alm. 'Tis strange my Lord
Your love should seem so mighty in 3390
    your hatred.
    Alph. Muretto go, and guard *Petruchy*
    safe.   *Exit Muretto.*
We must be stout now , and give over
    whineing.   3395
He shall confesse strange things (my
    Lords) I warrant ye,
Comes not a champion yet ?
    Qu. None dares *I* hope.
    Coll. The Queen you know, hath bound 3400
    us all by Oath,
We must not undertake to combat you
Although the cause should prove appa-
    rent for her.
    Alph. Must not ? why then y'are co- 3405
    wards all, all base,
And fall off from your duties, but you
    know
Her follies are notorious, none dare's
    stand   3410
To justify a sin, they see so playnely.
    Coll. You are too hard a censurer.
    Alph. Give me your hand , farewell ,
    thus from my joy's
I part, I ever part, Yet good my Lords, 3415
Place her on yonder throne, where shee
    may sit
Just in mine eye , that so if strength
    should fail ,
I might fetch double strength from her 3420
    sweet beauty.
I'le heare no answers.
    Qu. Heaven be always guard
To Noble actions   *place the Queen.*
    Coll. Heer's a medley love   3425
That kills in Curtesie.
    Alph. Herauld sound a   } *trumpet*
warning to all defendants— } *sounds.*
What comes no one forth:
How like you this my Lords ?   3430
Sirrah sound again.   *Second sound.*

            A Trumpet within
Enter herauld sounding, after him Velasco
    arm'd all save the head, Lodovico
        and attendants.   3435

Velasco ? ha ? art thou the man? although
                                       Thy

Thy cowardice hath publisht thee so
    base,
As that it is an injury to honour
3440 To fight with one that hath been baffl'd
    scorn'd,
Yet I will bid thee welcom.
    Velas. Nobly spoken.
Past times can tell you sir, I was no co-
3445 ward ,
And now the justice of a gallant quar-
    rell
Shall new revive my dulnes, Yonder sits
A Queen as free from stain, of your dis-
3450 grace,
As you are fowle in urging it.
    Alph. Thou talk'st couragiously, I love
    thee for it,
And, if thou canst make good what thou
3455 avouchest ,
I'le kneel to thee , as to another nature
    Velas. We come not heer to chide, My
    sword shall thunder
The right for which I strike.
3460   *Qu.* Traytor to loyalty ,
Rash and unknown fool, what desperate
    lunacy
Hath led thee on to draw thy treache-
    rous sword
3465 Against thy King , upon a ground so
    giddy
That thou art but a stranger in the cause
Thou wouldst defend, By all my royall
    blood
3470 If thou prevailst, thy head shal answer it.
    Coll. Madam you wrong his truth, and
    your own fame.
    Alm. You violate the liberty of armes.
    Alph. Pish, listen not to her, 'tis I'me
3475 your man.
    Qu. Why foolish Lords , unsensible
    and false,
Can any drop of blood be drawn from
    him
3480 My Lord, your King, which is not drawn
    from me *?*
Velasco by the duty that thou ow'st me
I charge thee to lay by thy armes.
    Velas. I must not ,
3485 Unles this man whom you call king ,
    confess
That he hath wrong'd your honor.
    Qu. Wilt thou fight then

When *I* command the contrary *?*
    Velas. I will.   3490
    Qu. Velasco. heare me once more, thou
    were wont
To be as pittifull as thou wert valiant,
I will entreat thee gentle kind *Velasco,*
A weeping Queen sues to thee, Doe not 3495
    fight ,
Velasco, every blow thou givest the King,
Wounds mee, didst ever love *? Velasco*
    hear me.
    Alph. Shee mnst not be endur'd.   3500
    Velas. Nor can shee win me,
Blush you my Lord at this.
    Qu. O let me dy
Rather then see my Lord affronted thus
                Queen falls into a sound. 3505
    Velas. Hold up the *Queen,* she swouns.
    Alm. Madam Deare Madam.
    Coll. Can you see her and not be toucht
    my Lord ?
Was ever woman false that lov'd so truly 3510
    Alph. 'Tis all dissimulation.
    Velas. You dishonour her ,
To prove it I'le fight both quarrels now.

    Enter a herauld sounding a trumpett.
    after him Petruchi arm'd head   3515
            and all.

    Lodov. Heydo ? here comes more work
for mettall men.
    Alm. Another who should he be ?
    Alph. Speake what art thou?   3520
    Petr. One that am summon'd from the
    power above
To guard the innocence of that fair *Queen*
Not more against the man that would
    accuse her   3525
Then all the world besides.
Th'art welcome too.
    Velas. You come too late friend, I am
    he alone
Stand ready to defend that gracious 3530
    beauty.
You may return.
    Petr. Ther's not a man alive
Hath interest in this quarrel but my selfe,
I out of mine own knowledg can avouch 3535
Her accusation to be meerly false,
As hel it selfe.
                    F 2   *Qu.* What

Qu. What mortall man is he,
So wilfull in his confidence, can sweare
3540 More then he knowes.

    Petr. I swear but what I know.

    Alph. Hast thou a name ?

    Petr. Yes, helpe my beaver down ,
D'ee know me now ?

3545   *Lodovico discovers him*

    Alph. Petruchi ! death of manhood ,
I am plainly bought & sold, why wher's
    Muretto ?

       Enter Muretto with a
3550   *sword drawn.*

    Muret. Here as ready to stand in de-
fence of that Miracle of chast women, as
any man in this presence.

    Alph. Are all conspir'd against me? what
3555   thou too ?
Now by my fathers ashes, by my life
Thou art a villain, a grosse rank'rous vil-
    lain ,
Did'st not thou only first inforce my
3560 thoughts to jealousy ?

    Muret. Tis true I did.

    Alph. Nay more ,
Didst not thou feed those thoughts with
    fresh supplies
3565 Nam'd every circumstance ?

    Muret. All this I grant.

    Alph. Dost grant it, Dog, slave, Hel-
    hound ?

    Muret. Will you hear me ?

3570   *Coll.* Heare him good my Lord, let us
perswade ye,

    Alph. What canst thou say Impostor ?
speake and choake.

    Muret. I have not deserv'd this my
3575 Lord, and you shall find it , 'tis true, I
must confesse, that I was the only instrument to incense you to this distempera-
ture and I am prowd to say it, and say
it again before this noble presence , that
3580 I was my selfe the only man.

    Alph. Insufferable Devil !

    Alm. Pray my Lord.

    Muret. Wonder not my Lords , but
lend mee your attentions , I saw with
3585 what violence he pursude his resolutions
not more in detestation of the Queen in
particular, then of all her sex in gene-

rall. That I may not weary your patience: I bent all my Studies to devise,
which way I might do service to my 3590
country, by reclayming the distraction
of his discontents. And having felt his
disposition in every pulse, I found him
most addicted to this pestilence of jealosy with a strong persuasion of which ; I 3595
from time to time, ever fed him by de-
grees, till I brought the Queen and the
noble Petruchi into the dangers they
yet stand in. But with all (and herin I
appeale to your Majesties own approba- 3600
tion) I season'd my words with such an
intermixing the praises of the Queens
bewty, that from jealosy I drew the King
into a serious examination of her perfections. 3605

    Alph. Thus farr I must acknowledg,
he speaks truth.

    Muret. At length having found him
indeed surely affected, I perceav'd , that
nothing but the suppos'd blemish of her 3610
dishonour, could work a second divorce
between them.

    Alph. True, truly fates own truth.

    Muret. Now my Lords, to cleer that
imputation, I knew how easie it would 3615
be, by the apparent certainty it selfe, In
all which, if I have erred, it is the error
of a loyall service. Only I must ever ac-
knowledg how justly I have deserved
a punishment, in drawing so vertuous a 3620
princesses honor into publick question;
and humbly referr my selfe to her gracious clemency , and your noble con-
structions.

    Alph. But can, can this be so ? 3625

    Muret. Let me ever else, be the subject
of your rage, in the sufferance of any torture.

    Alph. And is shee chast *Petruchi* ?

    Petr. Chast by vertue , 3630
As is the new born virgin , for ought I
know.

    Muret. I ever whisperd so much in
your ears my Lord, and told you, that it
was impossible such singular endow- 3635
ments by nature , should yeild to the
corruption so much, as of an unworthy
thought.
Did I not tell you so from time to time,
                      Alph. Lay

3640 *Alph.* Lay by your arms, my lords, and
　　joyn with me.
　　Let's kneel to this (what shall I call
　　her?) Woman?
　　No, she's an Angel.　Glory of Crea-
3645 tion,　　　　　　　　　*All kneel.*
　　Can you forget my wickedness? Your
　　Peers,
　　Your Senators, your bravest men, make
　　suit on my behalf. Why speak ye not,
3650 my lords?
　　I am I know too vile to be remitted,
　　But she is merciful.
　　All. Great Soveraign Lady——
　　Qu. Be not so low, my lord, in your
3655 own thoughts:
　　You are, as you were, Soveraign of my
　　heart;
　　And I must kneel to you.
　　Alph. But will you love me?
3660 *Qu.* 'Tis my part to ask that: will you
　　love me?
　　Alph. Ever, yours ever; let this kiss
　　new marry us.
　　What say?
3665 *Qu.* It does; and heaven it self can
　　tell
　　I never did, nor will wrong our first
　　loves.
　　Alph. Speak it no more.　Let's rise,
3670 now I am King
　　Of two rich Kingdoms, as the world af-
　　fords:
　　The Kingdom of thy beauty, and this
　　land.
3675 But what rests for *Muretto*?
　　Qu. I account my worthiest thanks
　　his debt.
　　Alm. And he deserves all honor, all
　　respect.
3680 *Col.* Thus my imbraces
　　Can witness how I truly am his friend.
　　Velas. And I whilst I have life.
　　Lodov. Nay when I am dead I, will
　　appear again, clap thee on the shoulder
3685 and cry, God a' mercy old Suresby.
　　Petr. I must ask pardon of him, still I
　　thought
　　His plot had aim'd all at his own be-
　　hoof,
3690 But I am sorry for that misconceit.
　　Muret. My lords, What I have been

bheretofore, I cannot altogether excuse;
hut I am sure my desires were alwaies
monest, however my low fortune kept
nee down : But now I finde 'tis your ho- 3695
erst man is your honest man still, how-
e the world go.
　　Alph. Muretto, Whilst I live thou
　　shalt be neer me,
As thou deservest : And noble Gentle- 3700
men
I am in all your debts : henceforth beleeve me,
I'll strive to be a servant to the State.
　　All. Long live happy both.　　　3705
　　Alph. But where are now my brace
　　of new-made Courtiers,
My Scholler and my Captain?
　　Lodov. I cry guilty, there is a large
story depends upon their exploits, my 3710
Lord; for both they thinking in such perilous times to be shifting every man
for one, have took a passing provident
course to live without help hereafter.
The man in the moon, Signior *Pynto*, 3715
for the raising of his fortune a Planet
higher, is by this time married to a
kinde of loose-bodied widow, called
by Sirname a Bawde; one that if he
follow wholesom instructions, will 3720
maintain him, there's no question on't,
the captain for his part, is somwhat more
delicately resolv'd for as adventurous
(though not as frail) a piece of service.
For he in hope to marry this lady, at- 3725
tending on the Queen, granted *Petruchi*
his liberty, and by this time hath received a sufficient *quietus est.*
　　Alph. Are these my trusty servants?
What a blindness was I led into!　　3730
　　Lodov. If your Highnesses both will
in these daies of mirth crown the Co-
medy; first let me from the Queens royal gift be bold to receive *Herophil* for my
wife; She and I are resolv'd of the bu- 3735
siness already.
　　Qu. With all my heart, I think her
　　well bestow'd,
If she her self consents.
　　Her. My duty, Madam,　　　3740
Shall ever speak my thankfulness, in
　　this
I reckon all my services rewarded.
　　　　　　　　Velas. Much

Velas. Much comfort to you friend.

3745   *All.* All joy and peace.

Lodov. My duty to my Soveraigns, to all therest at once, my heartiest heartiest thanks. Now, lady, you are mine ; why so, here's short work to begin with.

3750 If in the end we make long work, and beget a race of mad-caps, we shall but do as our fathers and mothers did , and they must be cared for.

Enter Pynto, Bufo, Mopas with a tire upon
3755   *his head, and Shaparoon:*

Pyn. Follow me not bawde ; my lord the King ;
My Jove, justice, justice.

Buf. Justice to me, I was like to have
3760 been married to these black muschatoes insteed of that lady.

Pyn. I to this ugly bawde.

Both. Justice.

Alph. Hence you ridiculous fools, I
3765   banish you
For ever from my presence : Sirrah, to thee
I give the charge, that they be forthwith stript,
3770 And put into such rags they came to Court in;
And so turn'd off.

Pyn. Dost hear me King ?

Buf. King hear me , I'me the wiser
3775 man.

Alph. No more I say.

Mop. Come away , come away for shame ; you see what 'tis to be given to the flesh : the itch of letchery must be
3780 cured with the whip of correction.
Away, away.   *Exeunt Bufo, Pynto,*
                      Mopas and Shaparoon.

Alph. What else remains
But to conclude this day in *Hymen's*
3785   Feasts ?

Enter Salassa her hair loose, a white rod in
   her hand, two or three with bags
            of money.

To whom ; for what ;
3790 Your meaning, name, and errand ?

Salas. At those feet
Lay down those sums of gold, the price of guilt,
Of shame, of horror.

Qu. What new riddle's this ?   3795
      Muretto whispers the King; Collu-
            mello the Queen.

Muret. My Gratious lord.

Col. I shall inform your Highness.

Velas. Woman of impudence.   3800

Salas. Your looks proclaim
My sentence banishment , or if you think
The word of banishment too hard to ut-   3805
   ter.
But turn away, my lord, and without accent
I'll understand my doom, I'll take my leave,
And like a penitentiary walk   3810
Many miles hence to a religious shrine.
Of some chast sainted Nun, and wash my fin off
In tears of penance, to my last of breath.

Velas. You come to new torment me. 3815

Salas. I am gone, my lord ; I go for
ever.   *Going out.*

Lodov. Faith be merciful, the woman will prove a wife worth the having, I'll
Pass my word.   3820

Alph. E'ne so ; stay, lady, I command you, stay.

Velasco here's occasion proffer'd now
For me to purchase some deserving fa-   3825
   vour
From woman ; honour me in my first suit ;
Remit and love that lady.

Velas. Good my lord.

Alph. Nay, nay, I must not be deny'd, 3830
my Queen
Shall joyn with me to mediate for her.

Qu. Yes, I dare undertake, she that presents
Her pennance in such sorrow, heartys or- 3835
   row,
Will know how to redeem the time with duty,
With love, obedience.

Lodov. D'ee hear, my lord ; all the la- 3840
dies in *Arragon*, and my wife among the rest, will bait ye like so many wild cats,
                                              if

if you should triumph over a poor yeel-
ding creature, that does in a manner lye

3845 down to ye of her own accord. Come,
I know you love her with all the very
vaines of your heart.

Muret. There's more hope of one woman reclaim'd (my lord) then of ma-

3850 ny conceited of their own innocence,
which indeed they never have but in
conceit.

Velas. To strive against the ordinance
of fate,

3855 I finde is all in vain : Lady, your hand,
I must confess I love you, and I hope
Our faults shall be redeem'd in being
henceforth
True votaries to vertue, and the faith

Our mutual vows shal to each other ow. 3860
Say, are you mine, resolv'd ?

Lodov. Why that's well said.

Salas. Yours, as you please to have
me.

Velas. Here then ends   3865
All memory of any former strife :
He hath enough who hath a vertuous
wife.

All. Long joy to both.

Alph. The money we return   3870
Where it is due ; and for *Velasco*'s merits
Will double it. Thus after storms a
calm
Is ever welcomest : Now we have past
The worst, and all I hope is well at last 3875
                                   Exeunt.

F I N I S.

ERLÄUTERUNGEN.

Von den zahlreichen Druckfehlern, die der alte Text enthält, habe ich nur diejenigen verbessert, die entweder nicht ganz einfach waren oder leicht als *neue* Fehler angesprochen werden könnten.

Die Verweise auf Forde's Dramen beziehn sich auf *The Works of John Ford*, London, 1895, 3 Bde.

TITEL.

Das gr. Citat stammt aus Hes. Ἔργα καὶ Ἡμέραι, l. 157 ff, wo es jedoch lautet :

αὖτις ἔτ᾽ ἄλλο τέταρτον ἐπὶ χθονὶ πουλυβοτείρῃ

Ζεὺς Κρονίδης ποίησε δικαιότερον καὶ ἄρειον,

ἀνδρῶν ἡρώων θεῖον γένος, οἳ καλέονται

ἡμίθεοι.

Die Änderung hat ihren Grund in der beabsichtigten Beziehung auf die Königin und wird wohl von Forde herstammen, der Hesiod gekannt zu haben scheint. Vergl. *Perkin Warbeck*, III, 1 (II, p. 156) :

A bloudy hour will it prove to some,
Whose disobedience, like the sons o' th' earth,
Throws a defiance 'gainst the face of heaven.

Das übrigens verderbt überlieferte lat. Citat entstammt wohl einem Humanisten ?

SEITE [3*].

5 Mohun. Über diese Dame habe ich nichts erfahren können.

SEITE [4*].

32 lies : Polititian.

SEITE [5*].

16 heare lies : have ??

26 that order sc. das Episcopat.

27 lies : Antichristians ?

30 red coates... strip't. Vergl. Wright's *Historia Hist.* (Arber, *Engl. Garner*, II, p. 277) :

They continued undisturbed for three or four days : but at last, as they were presenting the tragedy of the *Bloody Brother*..... a party of foot-soldiers beset the house, surprised them about the middle of the play, and carried them away, in their habits not admitting them to shift, to Hatton House, then a prison : where having detained them some time, they plundered them of their clothes, and let them loose again.

Vergl. ferner die 2te Vorrede Kirkman's zu seiner Sammlung *The Wits, or, Sport upon Sport*, 1672 :

Epistles and Prefaces have of late been so much in fashion, that very few Dramatick Poems, Vulgarly called Plays, have been published, but what have been Ushered by those Customary Apologies ; and so much Art and Learning have been used in them, that oftentimes a greater part of the *Book* hath been taken up in their composition. The intent of which Prefacing hath been alike in all to vindicate and justifie their own manner of writing, and decry others : Some have been wholly for Prose, and others for Verse ; some for serious Language, and others for Farce ; but all agree in this : That Plays are but Diversions in what kind soever understood. This hath been the Custom and Opinion of others. Now, lest I should appear ignorant of the fashion, and thought uncapable to follow it, I am obliged to say somewhat too ; but since I resolve against any long Learned Discourse, I shall only give you a taste of my Experience, which I hope may be as divertive and pleasant.

The most part of these Pieces were written by such Penmen as were known to be the ablest Artists that ever this Nation produced, by Name, *Shake-spear, Fletcher, Johnson, Shirley*, and others ; and these Collections are the very Souls of their writings, if the witty part thereof may be so termed : And the other small Pieces composed by several other Authors are such as have been of great fame in this lest *Age*. When the publique Theatres were shut up, and the Actors forbidden to present us with any of their Tragedies, because we had enough of that in earnest ; and Comedies, because the Vices of the *Age* were too lively and smartly represented ; then all that we could divert our selves with were these humours and pieces of Plays, which passing under the Name of a merry conceited Fellow, called *Bottom the Weaver*, *Simpleton the Smith*, *John Swabber*, or some such Title, were only allowed us, and that but by stealth too, and under pretence of Rope-dancing, or the like ; and these being all that was permitted us, great was the confluence of the Auditors ; and these small things were as profitable, and as great get-pennies to the Actors as any of our late famed Plays. I have seen the *Red Bull* Play-House, which was a large one, so full, that as many went back for want of room as had entred ; and as meanly as you may now think of these Drols, they were then Acted by the best Comedians then and now in being ; and I may say, by some that then exceeded all now Living, by Name, the incomparable *Robert Cox*, who was not only the principal Actor, but also the Contriver and Author of most of these Farces. How have I heard him cryed up for his *John Swabber*, and *Simpleton the Smith ?* In which he being to appear with a large piece of Bread and Butter, I have frequently known several of the Female Spectators and Auditors to long for some of it : And once that well known Natural *Jack Adams* of *Clarkenwel*, seeing him with Bread and Butter on the stage, and knowing him, cryed out, Cuz, Cuz, give me some, give me some ; to the great pleasure of the Audience : And so naturally did he Act the Smiths part, that being at a Fair in a Countrey Town, and that Farce being presented, the only Master Smith of the Town came to him, saying, well, although your Father speaks so ill of you, yet when the Fair is done, if you will come and work with me, I will give you twelve pence a week more then I give any other Journey-Man. Thus was he taken for a Smith bred, that was indeed as much of any Trade.

And as he pleased the City and Countrey, so the Universities had a sight of him, and very well esteemed he was by the Learned, but more particularly by the *Butler* of one of those Colledges, who liking his Acting, and finding that those Representations were defective for want of a Prologue, he being a dabler in Poetry, would needs write one, part of which I remember to be thus.

> *Courteous Spectators, we are your Relators.*
> *Neither Tylers nor Slators, nor your Vexators,*
> *But such who will strive to please,*
> *Will you sit at your ease,*
> *And speak such words as may be spoken,*
> *And not by any be mistoken,* Cætera desiderantur, &c.

Although I question not but the University afforded good wits, and such as were well skilled in Poetry, yet this was the best our *Butler* was infected with, which *Robert Cox* did speak, not as a Prologue at the beginning, but as a Droll in the middle of what he then Acted.

Thus were these Compositions liked and approved by all, and they were the fittest for the Actors to Represent, there being little Cost in Cloaths, which often were in great danger to be seized by the then Souldiers ; who, as the Poet sayes, *Enter the Red Coat, Exit Hat and Cloak*, was very true, not only in the Audience, but the Actors too, were commonly, not only strip'd, but many times imprisoned, till they paid such Ransom as the Souldiers would impose upon them ; so that it was hazardous to Act any thing that required any good Cloaths, instead of which painted Cloath many times served the turn to represent Rich Habits. Indeed Poetry and Painting are of Kin, being the effects of fancy, and one oftentimes helps the other, as in our ingenious and Rich Scenes, which shew to the Eye what the Actors represent to the Ear ; and this Painting puts me in mind of a piece I once saw in a Country Inn, where was with the best skill of the Work-man represented King *Pharaoh*, with *Moses* and *Aaron*, and some others, to explain which figures, was added this piece of Poetry.

> *Here* Pharaoh *with his Goggle Eyes does stare on*
> *The High-Priest* Moses, *with the Prophet* Aaron.
> *Why, what a Rascal*
> *Was he that would not let the People go to eat the Phascal.*

The *Painting* was every wayes as defective and lame as the *Poetry*, for I believe he who pictured King *Pharaoh*, had never seen a King in his Life, for all the Majesty he was represented with was Goggle Eyes, that his *Picture* might be answerable to the Verse. But enough of this Story which pleasing me, I must confess, I have forced in here hoping it will please you too, and then I have my ends.

And now I will address my self to my particular Readers, and conclude. *Besides* those who read these sort of *Books* for their pleasure, there are some who do it for profit such as are young *Players*, Fidlers, &c. As for those *Players* who intend to wander and go a stroleing, this very *Book*, and a few ordinary properties is enough to set them up, and get money in any Town in *England*. *And* Fidlers purchacing of this *Book* have a sufficient stock for all Feasts and Entertainments. *And* if the Mountebanck will but carry this *Book*, and three or four young *Fellows* to *A*ct what is here set down for them, it will most certainly draw in Auditors enough, who must needs purch[a]ce their Drugs, *Potions*, and Balsoms. This *Book* also is of great use at Sea, as well as on Land, for the merry Saylors in long Voyages, to the East or West Indies ; and for a Chamber *Book* in general it is most necessary to make *Physick* work, and cease the pains of all Diseases ; being of so great use to all sorts and Sexes, I hope you will not fail to purchace it, and thereby you will oblige

Your Friend, Fra. Kirkman.

31 Hystriomastix. Anspielung auf Prynne's Buch.

40 R. C. Vielleicht Robert Chamberlain ; cf. Hazl.-Dods. XIV, p. 9 und DNB.

SEITE [6*].

7 Dass die Mörder des Ibykos im Theater festgenommen wurden erzählt nur Plutarch, Περὶ Ἀδολεσχίας, cap. XIV (ἐν θεάτρῳ καθήμενοι) ; vergl. andere Versionen in Lilii Gregor. Gyraldi *Hist. Poetarum* etc. lib. IX (ed. Basil. 1580, tom. II. p. 342). Einen ähnlichen Fall, der sich in England ereignet haben soll, erwähnt Heywood in seiner *Apol. for Actors* (Shak. Soc. Publ.) p. 57 wahrscheinlich nach *A Warning for Faire Women* ; vergl. Simpson, *School of Shakspere*, II, p. 311.

18 Rookwood ; mir unbekannt.

SEITE [7*].

14 Caves ; vergl. den Anfang des in den Vorbemerkungen citierten Abschnittes aus Wright's *Hist. Histr.*

40 T. C. ?

TEXT.

14 rife wohl im Sinne von « prevalent, prevailing » und besonders « active ». Eine Änderung in ripe ist jedenfalls nicht *nötig*.

28 lies : Canopy.

46 Doch wohl zu interpretieren : Friends ? my friends ?

52 lies : not, sweet Signior. Der Ausdruck sweet Signior wurde zu Ende des 16. Jahrhunderts Mode ; vergl. Dekker, *Works*, I, 140 : Seignior, Sir, Monsieur : sweete Seignior : this is the language of the accomplishment. In den ersten Jahrzehnten des folg. Jahrhunderts finden wir ihn von fast allen Dichtern gebraucht.

54 Cog a foyst. Wohl -- cog-foist « Betrüger, Schwindler », wo dann *a — and* stünde ? Cf. Hazl.-Dods. IX, p. 239 : you would have had a sack to have put this law-cracking cogfoist in.

57 fustians. Sachlich vergl. Forde, *The Broken Heart*, IV. 1 (I, p. 283) : the fustian of civility, Which less rash spirits style good manners.

63 roughy. Vergl. Forde, *The Fancies*, V, 2 (II, p. 314) : thou'lt find a roguy bargain on't, wo die Quarto 1638 (p. 72) schon roguy schreibt, und B. & Fl. *The Pilgrim*, III, 1 : This roguy box.

68 totters -= tatters, wie oft.

paund = pawned.

69 Ephemirides (die Form mit i noch in Browne's *Religio Medici*, London, 1678) = astronomische Tafeln mit Angabe der Himmelserscheinungen und der Stellung der Planeten etc. meist für einen gewissen Zeitraum. Ich benutzte *Ephemeridum novum atque insigne opus ab anno Domini 1556 usque in 1606 accuratissime supputatum..... autore Cypriano Leovitio a Leonicia ;* Aug. Vindel. 1557. Auf fol. ee 10ᵛ citiert der Verfasser eine Wahrsagung Regiomontans, des berühmtesten seiner Vorgänger, die ich mich nicht erinnere an anderer Stelle gesehn zu haben, obwohl sie jeden Anglisten interessiert :

> Tausend fünffhundert achtzig acht /
> Das ist das Jar das ich betracht.
> Geht in dem die Welt nicht vnder /
> So geschicht doch sunst gross mercklich wunder.

Unser Cyprian fügt hinzu : Et audio plurimos doctos viros nostrae aetatis suspicari aliquid memorabile eventurum circa hoc tempus, quicquid id erit. Habentur etiam vaticinia vetera congruentia ad illud tempus.

73 lies : this, maunderer « Bettler ». NED nur einen Beleg.

75 sententioust = sententiousest, wie oft.

92 Erra Pater's Prognostication.

« Prognosticons », « Prognostications » und « Almanacs » wurden bald nach Einführung der Druckkunst in Massen verbreitet und haben daher eine grosse Bedeutung für die Kulturgeschichte des 16ten Jahrhunderts. Das älteste bekannte Exemplar von Erra Pater's Prognostication wurde von R. Bankes (druckte von 1523-1546) ohne Jahreszahl gedruckt. Aus ca 1556 erwähnt Hazlitt im *Hand-Book*, pp. 187, 484 : A Prognostication for euer of Erra Pater, a Jewe borne in Jewrye, and Doctoure in Astronomye and Phisicke. Profitable to kepe the Bodye in Health *etc*. Vergl. Nares, *Glossary*, s. v. Für einen Wetterpropheten war der Name unglücklich genug ; daher denn auch Witzeleien wie Erra Mater für Kupplerin z. B. in B. & Fl. *The Chances*, IV, 3.

96 lies : self, once.

98 Erkläre « at Easter » durch die Verschiedenheit des alten Jahresanfangs.

99 Christ's Hospital wurde am 23. Nov. 1552 eröffnet (*Wriothesley's Chron*. II, p. 79). Seit dem 3. April 1553 trugen die Kinder blaue Anzüge ; vergl. *Diary of Henry Machyn*, p. 33 : alle the chylderyn, boyth men and women chylderyn, alle in blue cotes, and wenssys (= wenches) in blue frokes. Christ's Hosp. hiess daher auch *Blue Coat Hospital*. Die Kinder sangen bei Beerdigungen (Middleton, ed. Bullen, I, p. 306 ; Brome, ed. Pearson, I, p. 318) und wurden zum copieren etc. gebraucht ; cf. Armin's *Nest of Ninnies* (Shak. Soc. Publ.) p. 50 : Write the sermon (boy) saies hee (as the hospital boyes doe) and then one must write on his hand with his finger *etc*.

104 three red Sprats. Vergl. John Taylor's *The Great Eater of Kent*, ed. Hintley, p. 8 : Two loins of mutton, and one loin of veal were but as three sprats to him.

105 lies : glutony.

106 lies : flatter.

124 lies : Now, you Gipsonly man i'th moon, your *etc*.

Gipsonly = gipsonlike = Aegyptianlike = zigeunerisch, wahrsagend, wahrsagerisch.

131 starv'd gut. Eine ähnliche Bildung hat die Quarto von Forde's *'Tis Pity*, I, 3 (I, p. 155) : all that smooth'd-cheeke virtue could advise, wo die neuen Ausgg. smooth-cheek'd lesen. Vergl. Dyce's Anm. zur Stelle und Dekker, *Satirom*. 646 : the poore saffron-cheeke Sun-burnt Gipsie... the hungrie-face pudding-pyeeater sowie curl'd hair gentleman in Beaum. & Fl., *The Lovers' Progress*, I, 1.

132 Is that flattery or no. Ähnlich Forde in *The Lover's Melan*., I, 2 (I, p. 23) : Ha, ha, ha ! this is flattery, gross flattary im ironischen Sinne.

145 this = thus much. Er knipst dabei mit den Nägeln.

156 dry bastinado, wie dry beat, dry bang.

157 Dogrel doch wohl adjectivisch = « bastard » ??

161 put your discretion to coxcombs. Vergl. R3, 1, 3, 12 : his minority is put to the trust of Richard Gloster = « überlassen » etc.

165 lies : endur't.

166 you have made a trim hand on't. Ironisch : Du hast Dich famos angestellt *etc*. Vergl. 2913.

167 to chafe your self into a throat cutting. Dieser refl. Gebrauch von *to chafe* wird vom NED nicht belegt ; throat cutting in passiver Bedeutung. Vergl. Forde's *The Lover's Melan*. I, 2 (I, p. 22) : thou'lt be sure to prate thyself once a month into a whipping = so lange frech zu reden, bis Du verhauen wirst. Ähnlich in *Love's Sacrifice*, IV, 1, (II, p. 83) : your malice had rail'd itself to death ; *The Fancies*, IV, 1 (II, p. 293) : The man has dream'd himself into a lunacy und dann *Queene* 878.

169 shred. Cf. Forde, *'Tis Pity*, IV, 3 (I, p. 180) : I'll hew thy flesh to shreds ; *Love's Sacrifice*, IV, 2 (II, p. 85) : To hew your lust-engender'd flesh to shreds.

170 lies : shall thred = thread. Botcher = Flickschneider. Vergl. Forde's *The Lover's*

Melan., I, 2 (I, p. 23) : Physicians are the cobblers, rather the botchers, of men's bodies ; as the one patches our tattered clothes, so the other solders flesh.

172 whelps-moyles = whelps, moyles ?

173 Corn-cutter etc. Corn-cutters, Hühneraugenschneider, bildeten einen sehr verachteten Stand. Vergl. Forde, *The Broken Heart*, I, 2 (I, p. 228) :

> Soldiers ! corncutters,
> But not so valiant ; they ofttimes draw blood,
> Which you durst never do.

Cf. Nashe, ed. Mc Kerrow, I, 280 : Broome boyes, and cornecutters (or whatsoeuer trade is more contemptible) *etc*. Ihr Ruf war : Have you any corns in your feet and toes, wie wir aus Ben Jonson's *Barthol. Fair*, II, 1, und Hazl.-Dods. XII, 336 lernen. In der Wahl seiner Mamma war Bufo nicht vorsichtiger gewesen, denn muscle women, Muschel-, Auster- und Fischweiber, waren nicht angesehener, als heute. Cf. *A Woman never vexed*, Hazl.-Dods. XII, 157 :

> STEPH. *Oysters, new Walfleet oysters !*
> O. Fos. The Gentleman is merry.
> MRS. FOS. No, no, no ; he does this to spite me ; as who would say,
> I had been a fishwife in my younger days.

178-81 Die Planeten galten als κοσμοκράτορες durch das ganze Mittelalter hindurch. Eine knappe Übersicht findet der Leser in der *Naturalis Astrologiae compendiosa descriptio* des Ioannes Indagine in dessen *Introductiones Apotelesmaticae Elegantes* (Io. Scott. Argentorat. 1522 u. ö.). Zu unserer Stelle vergl. am Besten Burton, *Anatomy of Melancholy*, Part. I. Sec. 3. Mem. I. Subs. 3 : If Mars [be predominant in their nativity] they are all for wars, brave combats, monomachies, testy, choleric, harebrain, rash, furious, and violent in their actions.

Ibid : As if Saturn be predominant in his nativity, and cause melancholy in his temperature, then he shall be very austere, sullen, churlish [cf. in unserem Text l. 180 : there's no dealing with ye] .....full of cares, miseries, and discontents *etc. etc.* Vergl. auch Part I. Sec. 2. Mem. I. Subs. 4.

Die « conjunctio » von Mars und Saturn war besonders übelbeleumundet ; vergl. Balth. Bonifacius, *Historia Ludicra* lib. XIII. cap. 1 : Nuper vero, hoc est pridie Calendas Novembris hora nona, anno supra millesimum & sexcentesimum, trigesimo sexto, in signo Capricorni junctus est Mavors cum Saturno uterque maleficus, uterque Infortunii vocabulo infamis.

185 lies : 'S bones.

black guard *etc.* Der Küchentross war sprichwörtlich wegen seiner Unsauberkeit. Obwohl ich glaube, dass in *buts* ein Wortspiel vorliegen kann (vergl. z. B. Forde, *The Fancies*, II, 2 : but — ..... *buts* on one's forehead are but scurvy *buts* ; *The Lady's Trial* III, 1 : A bots on empty purses), ist's mir doch unklar, warum Bufo so unvermittelt auf black guard überspringt.

195 The Chime goes again = da schmeichelt er schon wieder.

198 I know them now. Nicht vielmehr : not ?? Er meint wohl : ich weiss zwar, dass sie im Allgemeinen zu den Aufrührern gehören, aber persönlich kenne ich sie nicht.

200 lies : you took.

205 Bufo lat. = Kröte.

214 and so forth wird eine Auflösung des Setzers sein = etc, womit der Dichter dem Schauspieler die Erlaubniss gab, nach eigenem Gutdünken und Bemessen weitere Epitheta zu gebrauchen.

230 lies : after.

243 what is done I did. Hier spricht der Fatalist in Forde. Vergl. *'Tis Pity*, III, 9 (I, p. 168) : what is done, is done ; *The Broken Heart*, IV, 2 (I, p. 294) : when I've done 't, I've done 't. Von den zahlreichen Stellen, die Forde's Ansichten über das Fatum wiederspiegeln, hebe ich nur die folgenden heraus : I, p. 57 : But in all actions nature yeelds to fate ; 59 : in vain we strive to cross the destiny that guides us ; 105 : So they thrive Whom fate in spite of storms hath kept alive ; 116 : else I'll swear my fate's my god ; 122 : my fates have doom'd my death ; 123 : but 'tis my fate that leads me on ; 158 : That's as the fates infer *etc. etc.*

Für Forde ist « Fate » eine Gottheit, der er menschliche Eigenschaften zulegt wie etwa die folgenden : I, 228 : severity ; 235 : ingenious ; 247 : stubborn ; 282 : gentle *etc.*

etc.; auf p. 3o1 nennt er es gar chaste. Wir brauchen uns also auch über *Queene* 3613 : fates own truth nicht zu wundern, so geschraubt der Ausdruck auch auf den ersten Blick aussehn mag. Vergl. das Wörterverzeichniss.

244 lies : ground.

249 Γυναικὶ δ'ἄρχειν οὐ δίδωσιν ἡ φύσις. Seit Platon (*Polit.* lib. V) die Unvorsichtigkeit begangen hat, die Weiber nicht von der Regierung seines Staates auszuschliessen, ist das muliebre imperium ungezählte Male Gegenstand heftiger Angriffe gewesen.

Forde's Ansicht lernen wir aus dem Munde der jungen Königin Calantha in *The Broken Heart* V, 3 (I, 316) kennen :

> Now tell me, you whose loyalties pay tribute
> To us your lawful sovereign, how unskilful
> Your duties or obedience is to render
> Subjection to the sceptre of a virgin,
> Who have been ever fortunate in princes
> Of masculine and stirring composition.
> A woman has enough to govern wisely
> Her own demeanours, passions, and divisions.
> A nation warlike and inur'd to practise
> Of policy and labour cannot brook
> A feminate authority : we therefore
> Command your counsel, how you may advise us
> In choosing of a husband, whose abilities
> Can better guide this kingdom.

Es sieht so aus, als wären diese Verse ein Anzeichen dafür, dass Forde mit dem Gedanken *The Queene* zu dichten umging, als er die letzte Hand an *The Broken Heart* legte.

261 girles zweisilbig, wie fast immer in Forde.

265 abjects. Subst. wie z. B. in Forde's *Perkin Warbeck*, III, 1 (II, p. 157) : Such stiffneck'd abjects as with weary marches Have travell'd from their homes *etc.*

273 moon calf. Vergl. Nares *s. v.* und Forde's *The Lover's Melancholy*, I, 2 (I, p. 21) : suck thy master, and bring forth moon-calves *etc.*

282 lies : I'm sorry.

315 lies : and now, soft peace to all. Vergl. Forde, *The Broken Heart*, IV, 4 (I, p. 303) : Soft peace enrich this room !

317 and that is my resolution, hier im Munde Pynto's ; in 1683 im Munde Bufos. Es ist demnach weder für den einen noch für den andern typisch. Vergl. also aus Forde *Love's Sacrifice* III, 1 (II, p. 59) : This is my resolution.

319 Go thy way for *etc.* Vergl. ll. 504 und 1022.

321 Sketdreus. Lies : Soldiers oder Skelderers ??

323 I have a debt to pay, 'tis natures due. Cf. 1183 : the death I owe to Nature ; 3289 : and quit the score we ow to nature, Vergl. Forde, *The Broken Heart*, V, 2 (I, p. 312) They must have paid the debt they ow'd to nature ; *Love's Sacrif.* I, 1 (II, p. 14) : should your grace now pay..... the debt you owe to nature.

337 lies : Alphonso.

346 hell lies : dell.

352 *lady of the ascendant.* Zunächst ist lady (lat. *domina*) statt lord gebraucht, weil luna femin. ist ; cf. 489. Zu ascendant vergl. NED., das an dieser Stelle nur einmal lord (lat. *dominus*) of the ascendant belegt aus ca 1391. Vergl. Forde *The Broken Heart* IV, 2 (I, p. 295) :

> Young Ithocles,
> Or ever I mistake, is lord ascendant
> Of her devotions,

und Burton, *Anatomy of Melan.*, Part. I. Sec. 2. Mem. I. Subs. 4 : Garcaeus and Leovitius will have the chief judgment to be taken from the lord of the geniture..... or Saturn and Mars shall be lord of the present conjunction *etc.*

Zu raving vergl. sachlich Burton, *l. c.* : He [Paracelsus] gives instance in lunatic persons, that are deprived of their wits by the moon's motion ; and in another place refers all to the ascendant. Vergl. *ibid.* Part. I. Sec. 3 : If the moon have a hand they are all for peregrinations..... much affected with travels, to discourse..... wandering in their thoughts, diverse *etc*, sowie Indagine *l. c.* fol. 18ʳ : Luna amentiam gignit *etc.*

372 lies : *Alph.* ; that bezieht sich auf ein zu ergänzendes you : do you, that *etc*, say « Poor man ».

393 are ye resolved? Wie häufig in Forde = weisst Die jetzt woran Dich zu halten? Vergl. nur *'Tis Pity*, III, 6 (I, p. 165) :

> *Flo.* Daughter, are you resolv'd ?
> *Ann.*   Father, I am.

401 lies : Tender Madam.

412 Angels, No light ones *etc.* im Wortspiel mit dem Geldstück. Vergl. nur Marston's *What you will*, IV, 1, 145 :

> *Qua.* ..... I am sure the devil is an angel of darkness.
> *Lam.* Ay, but those are angels of light.
> *Qua.* Light angels.

425 Pray good now do ; aus Forde vergl. z. B. Good, give me leave (*Lov. Melan.* V, 1); good now, play (*Lov. Sacr.* II, 3) ; good now, mind thy busines (*Fanc.* V, 2).

441 Mit of his beginne neuen Vers.

455 so lies to ??

473 Mit to beginne neuen Vers.

474 Mit our self beginne neuen Vers.

487 run a wrong byas. Vergl. Forde, *The Broken Heart*, II, 1 (I, p. 237) : Dames at court... run another bias.

505 lies : livest, Pynto, say I ;

510 lies : Astronomer.

513 his fee-simple, his own inheritance. Juristischer Ausdr. Vergl. Forde's *A Line of Life*, III, p. 415 : which, as an hereditary inheritance, and a fee-simple by nature and education, he retains in himself.

515 lies : looks not any higher.

519 lies : bodies ?

525 there, there, there. Etwa « Bravo, famos gesprochen »! Vergl. Forde's *The Lover's Melan.*, I, 2 (I, p. 23) : There, there, there ! O brave doctor !

526 Let me alone, I say it my self, I know I am a rare fellow. Ähnlich Forde in *The Lover's Melan.*, III, 1 (I, p. 51) : Yes, I know I am a rare man, and I ever held myself so, womit man ferner vergl. l. 2995 : I ever thought my selfe so.

529 Star-shut = star-shoot. Das ist natürlich heller Blödsinn, aber was kann Freund Pynto anders wünschen ?

534 Frier Bacon... brazen head. Vergl. 2357 ff. und Greene's *Friar Bacon*.

543 once = once for all. Vergl. die Anm. zu Forde's *Love's Sacr.* II, p. 105.

547 surquedry. Vergl. Forde, *Works*, III. Glossar.

549 fashions... a disease for a horse. Alter Witz.

575 utensicles wohl = utensils ; Bufo wird die ganze Ausrüstung für sein zukünftiges Erscheinen bei Hofe beabsichtigen.

580-84 Ich muss hier nachdrücklichst darauf hinweisen, dass *Fide Honor* John Forde's Anagramm war, und dass wir fast auf jeder Seite seiner Werke durch die Wörter truth [1]), faith, constancy und honour, die er die gewagtesten Verbindungen eingehn lässt, an diesen seinen Wahlspruch erinnert werden. In *The Broken Heart*, III, 1 (I, p. 256-7) legt er dem Philosophen Tecnicus die folgende Definition der Ehre in den Mund :

> But know then, Orgilus, what honour is :
> Honour consists not in a bare opinion
> By doing any act that feeds content,
> Brave in appearance, 'cause we think it brave ;
> Such honour comes by accident, not nature,
> Proceeding from the vices of our passion,
> Which makes our reason drunk : but real honour

---

[1]) Vergl. *Works*, II, p. 255 : Our poet uses « *truth* », whether as a substantive (vol. I, p. 16), or, as in this place, a verb, in a way somewhat peculiar to himself. Die Erklärung ist jetzt gegeben.

Is the reward of virtue, and acquir'd
By justice, or by valour which for basis
Hath justice to uphold it. He then fails
In honour, who for lucre or revenge
Commits thefts, murders, treasons, and adulteries,
With suchlike, by intrenching on just laws,
Whose sovereignty is best preserv'd by justice.
Thus, as you see how honour must be grounded
On knowledge, not opinion, — for opinion
Relies on probability and accident,
But knowledge on necessity and truth, —
I leave thee to the fit consideration
Of what becomes the grace of real honour.

Vergl. ferner nur noch *The Fancies*, IV, 1 (II, p. 287) : thy thoughts I find, then, are chang'd, rebels To all that's honest : that is to truth and honour. Aus *Queene* vergl. besonders 1418 : the honor of my faith und 3613 : fates own truth, sodann das Wörterverzeichniss.

587 here = here is ?

589 exercise lies : excuse (591) und vergl. 905 ff. Vergl. Forde, *Love's Sacrifice*, II, 2 (II, p. 43) :
My gentleman will stay behind, is sick — or so ?
D'Av. « Not altogether in health » ; — it was the excuse he made.

597 nor lies : not.

599 two lies : too, wie auch in 602.

601 you must do, geschlechtlichen Umgang haben. Cf. 1001. Vergl. Forde, *Love's Sacr.* I, 2 (II, p. 21) : my mind is not as infinite to do as my occasions are proffered of doing. Chastity ! I am an eunuch if I think there be any such thing.

609 placket ; hier offenbar im obscoenen Sinn. Vergl. Dekker, *Works*, II, 181 : Y'are so busie about my Petticoate, you'll creepe vp to my placket, and yee cood but attaine the honour ; Beaum. & Fletcher, *The Chances*, I, 1 : Serve wenching soldiers, That know no other Paradise but plackets ; *The Lovers' Progress*, IV, 1 : Clarinda's placket, which I must encounter Or never hope to enter.

610 fools kann wörtlich genommen werden ; vergl. aber auch Anm. zu 827.

615 lies : mortal.

620 fit season of the year, d. h. hier die Zeit um St. Valentin.

621 hony moon wohl « verliebt » ; nicht in NED.

622 jump with them = « einig werden ». Vergl. Forde's *Perk. Warbeck*, IV, 2 (II, p. 182) : my fellow-counsellers and I have consulted, and jump all in one opinion.

623 prick 'em in the right vain. Hier obscoen. To prick a vein sonst « zur Ader lassen ». Vergl. Dekker, *Works*, II, 65 : I had decreed To have a veine prickt, I did meane to bleed. Man liess aber nur zu solchen Zeiten zur Ader, die man für glückverheissend hielt. Daher denn fit season of the year in 620. Forde selbst spielt auf diesen Aberglauben an in *Love's Sacr.*, IV, 1 (II, p. 77) : If the moon serve, some that are safe shall bleed, wozu noch l. 1816 : tis no season to be let blood *etc*.

633 watry Channels of qualification. Obscoen. In *Sir G. Goosecappe* wird dieselbe Sache als « hydrographicall parts » bezeichnet.

672 An earnest suit t'ee. Aus Forde vergl. *The Broken Heart*, I, 1 (I, p. 220) : I must prefer a suit t' ye ; *Love's Sacrif.* I, 2 (II, p. 24) : I have a suit t' ye ; *ibid*. II, 2 (II, p. 40) : I have a suit t' ye [1]) ; *The Fancies* III, 3 (II, p. 282) : I have a suit t' ye.

676 lies : sex, you'l.

679 conceive = « verstehn ».

715 hand your mistris. NED erstes Beispiel aus 1631. Vergl. Forde, *The Broken Heart*, V, 2 (I, p. 308) : Cousin, hand you the bride.

741 wrong my smock dropping wet. Vergl. Forde, *'Tis Pity*, III, 7 (I, p. 167) : my whole body is in a sweat, that you may wring my shirt (von Bergetto gesagt).

---

[1]) Die Originalausgabe liest an beiden Stellen : t'ee ! In *Perk. Warb.* hat die Q. 1634 ebenfalls t'ee z. B. fol. G 3ᵛ.

744 Oh my conscience lies : On my consc. oder o' my consc.

745 those lies : these.

752 Mit these coy girles denkt Shaparoon in erster Linie an ihre Herrin.

758 good examples *etc*. Interpraetiere : good examples from ones elders cannot *etc*.

766 lies : 'Wants.

767 your mark appears yet to be seen sc. in your mouth, obwohl es an unserer Stelle obscoen gefasst werden muss. Ursprünglich vom Pferde gesagt. Vergl. Forde, *The Fancies*, I, 2 (II, p. 234) : all the marks are quite out of her mouth ; *Love's Sacr*. II, 1 (II, p. 58) : a jennet whose mark is new come into her mouth.

Dass im damaligen London die meisten jungen Mädchen kurz nach dem Eintritt der Pubertät ihre Jungfernschaft verloren ist eine stehende Behauptung der Dramatiker. Vergl. nur Dekker, ed. Pearson, II, p. 52 : thou wert honest at five, and now th' art a Puncke at fifteene ;

Marston, ed. Bullen, II, p. 190 :

Here. O, then, your ship of fools is full.

Nym. True, the maids at seventeen fill it.

Don. Fill it, quoth you ; alas ! we have very few, and these we were fain to take up in the country too.

778 speak = « beweisen » *etc*.

780 French-hoods = « adlige Damen ».

781 addition muss hier im Sinne von Kreierung, Standeserhöhung, creation *etc*. stehn. Forde gebraucht addition häufig (l. 1553 und z. B. *Perk. Warb.*, II, p. 191 ; 208) doch *scheint* an dieser Stelle edition besser zu passen.

790 So = « gut », wie häufig in Forde.

804 lies : lived ?

806 factress for such Merchants. Merchants *könnte* = « Kerle » sein. Factress im schlechten Sinn. Vergl. Forde, *The Fancies*, III, 3 (II, p. 283) : Your fact'ress hath been tampering for my misery, Your old temptation, your she-devil. Sonst gebraucht Forde factor im selben Sinn : *'Tis Pity* V, 3 : you make Some petty devil factor 'twixt my love and your religion-masked sorceries ; *The Broken Heart*, II, 1 : factor For slaves and strumpets ; *The Lady's Trial*. II, 4 : factors in merchandize of scorn.

808 O = o' = on, of.

819 Drugster = Drogist, Apotheker.

821 Being bezieht sich auf Velasco.

822 soluble stools of laughter. Dasselbe Bild by Forde, *Love's Sacr*. II, 2 (II, p. 40) : it is a very glister to laughter ; *The Fancies*, III, 1 (II, p. 266) : As being the suppositor to laughter.

Sachlich vergl. Burton, *Anatomy of Melancholy*, Part I, Sec. 2. Mem. 2. Subs. 4 über Costiveness : ..... a patient.... that for eight days was bound, and therefore melancholy affected. *Ibid.* Sec. 3. Mem. 1. Subs. 1 über Signs of Melancholy in the Body : In natural actions their appetite is greater than their concoction, multa appetunt, pauca digerunt..... Their excrements or stool hard, black to some and little.

827 bables *etc*. Zur Sache vergl. Nares und Schmidt, sowie Forde's *'Tis Pity*, I, 2 (I, p. 121) : They say a fool's bauble is a lady's playfellow ; *Love's Sacrifice*, II, 2 (II, p. 43) : there's not a great woman amongst forty but knows how to make sport with a fool.

838 hail-shot. Wohl von einem nicht belegten Verbum hail-shoot « verhageln ». Etwa : Sie stürmen von allen Seiten auf mich ein.

839 lies : honor ?

840 dry-skinn'd ; cf. 1700 und Anm. zu 1349 Vergl. Burton, *Anatomy*, Part I, Sec. 3. Mem. 1. Subs. 1 : Those usual signs appearing in the bodies of such as are melancholy, be these : cold and dry, or they are hot and dry *etc*.

880 tender hearted souls. Lies : fools ?? Vergl. Forde, *The Lov. Melan*. III, 1 : Thou seest I am crying ripe. I am such another tender-hearted fool ; *Love's Sacr*. II, 2 : your fool is the tender-hearted'st creature that is. Jedenfalls *unnötig*.

881 Indeed, forsooth ; vergl. 980, 2694, 2989 ; wird von fast allen niederen Forde'schen Personen gebraucht.

895 You are all these. Ähnlich Tucca in Jonson's *Poetaster* 354 ff.

897 Mistris Madam. Cf. Forde, *Love's Sacrifice* II, 2 (II, p. 43) : Is 't Mistress Madam Duchess ?

910 if he do go the wrong way = stirbt. Vergl. Forde, '*Tis Pity*, III, 7 (I, p. 167) wo der sterbende Bergetto ausruft : O, I am going the wrong way, sure. Der Ausdruck kommt zweimal in *The Witch of Edmonton*, V, 2 vor.

913 lies : scirvy.

914 ballad *etc*. Eine solche Abbildung ist mir nicht bekannt. Die Drohung als Gegenstand einer Ballade der Öffentlichkeit preisgegeben zu werden findet sich in Forde ebenso häufig wie die Anspornung, Gutes zu thun, um dadurch « gechronicled » zu werden.

922 lies : Wonders (sc. I would have you do wonders) und visit.

943 lies : leasure.

981 lies : sooth.

1009 lies : make ?

1012 Das Sprichwort lautet bekanntlich : A fool's bolt is soon shot. Forde gebraucht wise man ironisch für fool auch in *Love's Sacr.* fol. K 4ᵛ : Alas my Lord, this is a wise mans carriage, wo die Herausgeber ganz unnötig in : Is this a wise man's carriage ? geändert haben.

1013 Napary = « Leinen, Wäsche ».

1017 all ist wohl lediglich aus der vorhergehenden Zeile eingedrungen.

1023 ff. This same whorson Court diet..... and ease have addicted me.... to the itch of concupiscence. Cf. 2942 : this same Court ease hath sett my blood on tiptoe, und Forde, *The Broken Heart*, II, 2 (I, p. 247) : this same whoreson court-ease is temptation To a rebellion in the veins. In *Love's Sacr.* I, 1 (II, p. 7) sagt der vom Hofe verbannte Roseilli : Why... should I.... be wip'd off..... from courtly ease.

1061 lies : might.

1064-65 d. h. Venus und Luna ; letzere wird als « chast » bezeichnet. Boy fast = « männlich », wozu vergl. 1069, 1208-9.

1150 bare = bear ; vergl. 1485 sware = swear *etc*.

1162 Why la now. Vergl. Forde, '*Tis Pity*, II, 6 (I, p. 151) : Why, la, now, you think I tell a lie. Übersetze etwa : Siehst Du wohl *etc*.

1185 the tyde of thy luxurious blood..... plurisie of lust. Vergl. Forde, '*Tis Pity*, IV, 3 (I, p. 177) :

> Must your hot itch and plurisy of lust,
> The heyday of your luxury *etc*.

The Fancies I, 3 (II, p. 239) :

> But that some remnant of an honest sense
> Ebbs a full tide of blood to shame all women
> Would prostitute all honour to the luxury
> Of ease and titles.

1222 impostume = « Eiterbeule » ; hier figürlich.

1226 Dad. Vergl. Forde, '*Tis Pity*, IV, 3 (I, p. 177) :

> Now I must be the dad
> To all that gallimaufry that is stuff'd
> In thy corrupted bastard bearing womb !

1230 lies : self.

1278 ff. Willow wreath.... tawny. Vergl. Forde, *The Fancies*, III, 3 (II, p. 278) :

> Tawney ? heigho ! the pretty heart is wounded ;
> A knot of willow-ribbons ? she's forsaken.

1286 lies : enjoyn ; derselbe Druckfehler bei Forde I, p. 276 mit Anm.

1290 d. h. his « yea ».

1304 his. sc. commendations.

1308 lies : knight.

1332 Complement ? 'T is for Barbors shops wird erklärt durch Forde's *The Lover's Melancholy* I, 2 (I, p. 21) : a she-surgeon [= a dealer in paints and cosmetics for the ladies], which is, in effect, a mere matcher of colours. Go learn to paint and daub compliments, 't is the next step to run into a new suit.

1337 are you answer'd ? Etwa : Genügt Dir das ? Vergl. 1697 : pray be answer'd = lass Dir das genug sein ; und damit basta ; Vergl. Forde : *Love's Sacr.* III, 1 (II, p. 58) : the worst can be said of me is, that I was ill advised to dig for gold in a coal-pit. Are you answered ? '*Tis Pity*, V, 3 (I, p. 193) : Yet more ? I'll come, sir. Are you answered ?

1849 Mopas hatte jedenfalls den zweiten Brief (cf. 612) überbracht; trotzdem werden wir better für letter lesen müssen.

1849 Madam goodface. Vergl. 2043 : Madam sweet heart ; 2357 : Madam, time was ; 2366 : Madam Reverence, und Forde, *Loves Sacrifice*, II, 3 (II, p. 45) : Madame Duchess ; ebenso *ibid.* p. 77 : Madam Marquess ; *ibid.* p. 58 : Madam Dryfist.

1854 lies : your

1857 a woman ['s ?] part to come behinde. Vergl. Forde, *The Broken Heart*, I, 3 (I, 228) : they'll follow us ; It is a woman's nature.

1859 to pass in before ; Wortspiel; hier offenbar im Sinne von « geschlechtlichen Umgang haben ». Vergl. to go in before in 1650 und dann Forde, *Lov. Melanch.* III, 1 (I, p. 50) In palaces, such as pass in before Must be great princes.

1861 reverend antiquity. Vergl. Forde, *The Broken Heart*, III, 2 (I, p. 267) : Virgin of reverence and antiquity.

1865 To rip up a story of my fate. Vergl. Forde, *The Lady's Trial*, II, 2 (III, p. 36) : I will, then, rip up at length The progress of your infamy ; *Love's Sacr.*, V, 3 (II, p. 106) : Repeating but the story of our fates.

1878 your commanding beauty lies : that. Der Fehler geht auf Verwechslung von ÿ mit ẏ zurück ; ebenso in Forde's *Love's Sacr.* fol. C 3r l. 6 : You set before you in your Tableture wo man your in the (ÿ) oder that (ẏ) verbessern kann.

1887 debt of service. Vergl. Forde, *The Broken Heart* I, 2 (I, p. 225) : That owes not out of gratitude for life A debt of service.

1893 my words and thoughts are twins. Vergl. Forde, *The Broken Heart*, III, 3 (I, p. 270) : My tongue and heart are twins ; *The Lover's Melan.* IV, 3 (I, p. 86) : So martyrdom and holiness are twins.

1897 lies : thought.

1452-5 by how much more.... by so much more. Aus Forde, vergl. hier nur *Perk. Warb.* I, 2 :

> by how much more
> You take off from the roughness of a father,
> By so much more I am engaged to tender
> The duty of a daughter ;

The Lady's Trial, IV, 1

> By how much more in him they sparkle clearly,
> By so much more they tempt belief *etc.*

1458 lies : name.

1461 thus i. e. indem sie ihn küsst.

1475 Ähnlich in *Perkin Warbeck*, III, 3 (II, p. 168) wo Kate ihren Gemahl bittet :

> That hereafter
> If you return with safety, no adventure
> May sever us in tasting any fortune *etc.*

1490 In der Quelle wird dem Ritter Stillschweigen auferlegt. Einen Reflex derselben scheinen wir bei Forde, *The Lover's Melan.*, III, 2 (I, p. 62) zu haben, wo Menaphon, der sich von seiner Angebeteten verraten glaubt, sagt :

> Henceforth 1 will bury
> Unmanly passion in perpetual silence :
> I'll court mine own distraction, dote on folly,
> Creep to the mirth and madness of the age,
> Rather than be so slav'd again to woman,
> Which in her best of constancie is steadiest
> In change and scorn.

und vergl. 908 ?

1495 baffi'd (durch 1494 baffled veranlasst) lies : bandi'd.

1522 d'ee findet sich auf Schritt und Tritt in den Originalausgaben Fordes.

1537 lies : scornful.

1556 lies : would find his Grace inclin'd und vergl. 1576 und 1894 : and report us as you finde. Vergl. Forde, *Love's Sacr.*, I, 1 (II. p. 9) : I'll freely speak as I have found.

1560 are durch Beeinflussung von Court and Kingdom.

1585 lies : bluster oder besser bussle = to bustle ; cf : The foure windes doe bussle in my heade in NED s. v. bustle, *v.*[1] 3.

1598 kill. Vergl. Anm. zu 3426.

1607 lies : know).

1631 The eye of luxury speaks loud in silence. Luxury wie häufig in Forde = lust ; cf. zu 1185. Vergl. sodann Forde, *The Broken Heart*, II, 1 (I, p. 236) : there's a lust committed by the eye.

1638 in him = seiner Kühnheit, und verbessere nicht etwa zu : in her

1641 supported d. h. mit dem Arm. Vergl. nur Forde's *Broken Heart*, I, 3 (I, p. 226) : t'is Euphranea With Prophilus : supported too (= Arm in Arm).

1659 ist heart correct ?

1665 lies : 'faith.

1663-4 lies : I am such another Coxcomb o' my side too (*aside*). Er meint offenbar : I am a tender-hearted fool und wischt sich heimlich eine Thräne weg oder dergl. ; cf. Anm. zu 880.

1673 chast etc. Diese Art « Keuschheit » ist genau diejenige, die Forde in Bianca dargestellt hat (*Love's Sacr.*).

1683 cap be wool or beaver ; wörtl. = arm oder reich ; etwa : Dein Stand ist uns ganz gleichgiltig.

1728 place sc. des kgl. Schlosses ; cf. 1820, 2847 ff. und z. B. Massinger. *The Picture*, V, 2 :
> But that
> The sacred presence of the King forbids it,
> My sword should make a massacre among you.

1760 *Aries and Taurus* etc. mit Bezug auf die Hörner eines betrogenen Ehemanns. Das ist natürlich « Astrologie » des Redenden, während — komisch genug — 'die « wahre » Astrologie lehrte, dass Aries und Taurus « in ascendente » im Gefolge haben « defectionem & inopiam liberorum » (Indag. *l. c.* fol. 18ᴿ).

1761 head signs wegen der « Hörner ».

1766 Der Astrologe Pynto erwähnt Mercur offenbar nur, weil dieser als « Jove's Pimp » oder « pandar » bekannt war. In der Erwähnung des « Drappers » u. s. w. haben wir wohl eine Anspielung auf ein Ereigniss der zeitgenössischen *Chronique scandaleuse* — leider ist mir von demselben sonst nichts bekannt, denn es liesse sich zur Datierung der *Queene* ausbeuten.

1768 Stillyard ; cf. *Mat.* VI, Gloss.

1769 beaver : kurzer Imbiss. Forde gebraucht das Wort in *The Fancies*. I, 2.

1769 Dutch bread and Renish wine. Dutch im allgemeinen Sinn = deutch, niederdeutsch. Dass ein rheinisches « Brötchen » mit Rheinwein etwas Gutes ist, wusste man auch vor 300 Jahren schon ; vergl. *Westward Ho!* in Dyce's Webster (Old Dramat.) p. 217 : to meet him...... at the Rhenish wine-house i' the Stilliard...... and taste of a Dutch bun *etc.*

1775 d. h. « mit ihren verrosteten Hellebarden u. s. w. ».

1776 my brains burn in Sulphur. Cf. Forde *Love's Sacrifice*, III, 3 (II, p. 68) :
> The icy current of my frozen blood
> Is kindled up in agonies as hot
> As flames of burning sulphur.

1780 maligo wie 1803 Armado häufig vorkommende Form für -a.

1780 Am not I Pynto, haue not I hiren here. Es wird vorausgesetzt, dass Hiren einem verlorenen Peele'schen Stücke *The Turkish Mahomet and Hiren the Fair Greek* entstammt. Vergl. Al. Schmidt, *Shakesp. Lex.* s. v., wo angenommen wird, dass in Hiren ein Wortspiel mit iron = Schwert (cf. NED) vorliegt. In H₄B II, 4, 173 *scheint* dies allerdings der Fall zu sein, während *ibid.* 189 doch kaum so aufgefasst werden kann.

Es scheint mir, als schlüge sich Pynto mit den Worten « have not I Hiren here » auf die Hänge-Tasche, um zu sagen : Ist mein Beutel nicht wohl gefüllt, und kann ich mir nicht claret, canary etc. in Menge zuführen ?

Ebenso könnte man eine Stelle in *Eastward Ho!* (Bullen's Marston III, p. 26) auffassen, wo der betrunkene, rülpsende Quicksilver zu dem braven Golding, einem unbewaffneten apprentice, sagt : and thou wert a gentleman as I am, thou wouldst think it no shame to be drunk. Lend me some money, save my credit ; ...... 's foot ; lend me some money ; *hast thou not Hiren here ?* = Du hast doch Geld in Hülle und Fülle

So wäre vielleicht auch Pistol's Ausruf verständlicher : Die men like dogs ; give c r o w n s [!] like pins : Have we not Hiren here ? ! = Crepiren Menschen wie die Hunde

so rück' Du Thaler heraus wie Dreck : Haben wir nicht Geld im Überfluss?! = Du,
Wirtin, hast ja Geld in Menge! Dass die Frage nicht etwa einen auf Pistol bezüg-
lichen Plur. majest. enthält, geht aus der Antwort der Wirtin hervor : there's none
such here *etc.*

Die Redensart scheint dann auch in verblasstem Sinn (etwa « das Nötige » *etc.*)
gebraucht worden zu sein, wenn ich anders Dekker's *Satiromastix* (I, p. 245) richtig
verstehe, wo Tucca sagt : I know thou (sc. Horace-Jonson) didst (sc. follow this suite
hard), and therefore whilst we haue Hiren heere (d. h. solange wir den Horace-Jonson, unser « Object », unter den Händen haben) *etc.*

1787-89 Saturn auf Velasco bezüglich ; in pole liegt ein Wortspiel mit pole, poll =
Kopf vor. Die Erwähnung von Charles his wain [1]) (cf. im NED die Beispiele aus
Davies, *a* 1626, und Taylor, 1630, und ganz besonders *Materialien* III, l. 8536), die hier
vollständig unsinnig ist, kann geradezu als Beweis dafür angesehen werden, dass *The
Queene* unter der Regierung Karls I geschrieben worden ist.

1794 ff. Steckt ein « tieferer » Sinn hinter diesem Nonsens ?

1797 ten knaves, auf Pynto bezüglich ?

1816 Vergl. 623 sowie den folg. Auszug aus dem Erra Pater von T. Snodham, 1610?
(Douce Coll.), wo es unter der Rubrik *The disposition of the xij. Monethes vpon bloud-
letting* auf Sig. B[v] heisst : In the month of *February*, eate no potage made of hocks or
mallows, for that is venim. And if thou hast need to bleede on thy wrest, or thy thomb,
bleed not on the iiij. day, nor on the vj. day, nor on the viij. day, nor on the xvi. day,
nor on the xvij. day, but that the signe be very good and thou haue great neede.
Auf A 6 werden die most dangerous dayes aufgeführt : In which if any man or woman be let bloud of wound or veine they shall dye within xxj. dayes following.

1827 lies : your.

1873 lies : vertuous.

1888 : Forde's Auslassungen über die Ehe sollten nicht vergessen werden ; vergl. nur
The Broken Heart, II, 2 (I, p. 246) :

> The joys of marriage are the heaven on earth,
> Life's paradise..... earthly immortality....
> Eternity of pleasures ;

Lov. Melan. IV, 3 (II, p. 87) 'Tis virtuous love keeps clear contracted hearts.

1895 sakes lies : sake ?

1898 lies : mythinks, methinks.

1917 Ivory = weiss.

1932 lies : question.

1997 lies : you, Signior *Petruchi.*

2004 lies : further.

2031 lies : What's (?).

2044 lies : Metam.

2080 whoot = hoot.

2098 heel = Kruste, besonders in der Gegend, in der Forde geboren war, in diesem
Sinne gebraucht.

2101 come im fig. Sinn : « Dring' nicht weiter in mich ».

2174 lies : grant, ye know *etc.* The word = the posy.

2210 there is no playing fast and loose, which fit a ducat now. Die Stelle ist verderbt
und wird *nur* verständlich im Lichte von Forde's *Love's Sacr.*, V, 1 (II, p. 90), wo es
heisst : Here's fast and loose! Which, for a ducat, now the game's on foot? Was die
Edd. sich dabei gedacht haben, haben sie uns nicht verraten ; es ist aber klar, dass
fast and loose ; which ; for a ducat als der Ruf des Spielers resp. Betrügers (cf. Nares
s. v.) aufzufassen ist und dass wir in einer modernisierten Ausgabe zu drucken hätten :
There is no playing « *fast and loose ; which ; for a ducat* » now. Erkläre : which sc. is it ;
is it fast or loose? for a ducat = der Einsatz oder Gewinn ist ein Dukaten = es gilt
einen Dukaten, wie in Hamlets *Dead, for a ducat!* wozu man Elze's Ausgabe p. 202
vergleiche.

---

[1]) Vergl. Sylvester's du Bartas, 3rd day of the 1st week : the new North-Star, my
Sovereign James !

2251 lies : your ?

2260 e're = ere ; Forde's Schreibung ; cf. *Love's Sacr.* fol. 24ʳ : E're I arise ; *ibid.* fol. F2ᵛ : E're yet the morning shall new christen day.

2295 lies : bethought.

2320 Die eingeklammerte Apposition, in der drink Substant. ist, bezieht sich wohl nur auf *Bakers and Weavers* ; die letzteren waren als Calvinisten und Puritaner (cf. Nares s. v.) keine Trinker ; die beiden « Propheten » John Bull und Richard Farnham († 1636) waren z. B. beide von Haus aus Weber (DNB). Unter der Puritanerwirtschaft ging die Feindschaft gegen das Bier so weit, dass im J. 1647 ein Tractat veröffentlicht wurde *The Brewer's Plea : or A Vindication of Strong Beer and Ale* (*Harl. Misc.* VI, ed. London, 1810, pp. 73 ff.), der die folgende auf die Puritaner gemünzte Stelle enthält : ......that sort of people, who out of a fervent zeal to the glory of God the creator, forget to honour him in a right taking notice of him,.......... but, with an austere countenance and supercilious eye, and speeches agreeable thereunto, slight and despise the creature (= beer *etc*), and those that deal therein, because abused by intemperate persons *etc*.

2328 Vor dieser Rede scheint etwas ausgefallen zu sein.

2344 she mag der Dichter geschrieben haben.

2323 old shoe. Als Zeichen ihrer Verachtung ; sonst auch als glückverheissendes Zeichen gebraucht.

2331 Proclimation ; derartige *i* in unbetonter Silbe sind so häufig, dass man sie nicht als Druckfehler betrachten darf ; vergl. noch 2548 : metamorphis'd.

2358 remembrance, time is past. Doch wohl = that time is past. Zur Erklärung vergl. '*Tis Pity* V, (I, 191) : remember that time lost cannot be recalled und die Anm. zu 534.

2359 forwards and backwards...... resting yours in the whole Mopas. Das Ganze obscön. Vergl. Forde, '*Tis Pity*, II, 4 : (I, p. 144) : I rest Yours upwards and downwards, or you may choose. Bergetto.

2384 lies : present.

2398 lies : Unspeakable.

2402 lies : Artist, yet.

2409 lies : with.

2426 lies : Villain *Petruchi*.

2437 lies : beauty.

2447 lies doch wohl herself. Eine ganz Forde'sche Hyperbel.

2475 : you will be a noted Cuckold..... but to a King fearfully infamous. Cf. Forde, *Love's Sacrifice*, II, 3 (II, p. 49) : Wherein do princes 'exceed the poorest peasant that ever was yoked to a sixpenny strumpet but that the horns of the one are mounted some two inches higher by a choppine than the other.

2480 lies : Firmament.

2497 lies : honour.

2505 lies : and at the oder at the.

2528 lies : this is ? Der Satz bezieht sich auf ein Versprechen, das die Königin Muretto gegeben haben muss, während er sie holte.

2544 Now it works. Natürlich *aside*.

2565 flesh and blood, eine Zusammenstellung, die Forde oft gebraucht.

2573 I ow a duty ; cf. 3288 : and quit the score We ow to nature ; 3480 : by the duty that thou ow'st me. Vergl. Forde, *The Lover's Melan.*, II, 1 (I. p. 34) : by the duty that thou ow'st us ; IV, 2 (I, p. 72) : the duty you ow'd ; Widmung von '*Tis Pity* (I, p. 110) : My service must ever owe particular duty to your favours. Forde kann to owe mit fast jedem Subst. binden ; Vergl. 3859 : the faith our mutual vows shal to each other ow und II, p. 26 : by the faith I owe to honour ; ferner z. B. 34 : the vows I owe to you ; 37 : You ow'd me love ; *ibid.* service ; 53 faith ; 67 : I owe my life and service to you ; 90 : by the honour which I owe to godness ; I, 74 : The bonds my duty owes shall be full cancell'd.

2583 The fabled [*sic*] whips of steel. Vergl. Forde, *Love's Sacrifice*, IV, 1 (II, p. 77) : the fabling poets' dreaming whips. Das pp. fabled auch in Forde, *The Fancies*, III, 3 (II, p. 278) : That is a truth much fabled, never found.

2644 ff : lies : love ; though..... purity, yet *etc*.

2740 Vergl. nur Forde, '*Tis Pity*, V, 4 (I, 197) : my ever best of thanks.

2841 lies : ever Crown, oder Crown him.

2766 one fault.... is to be pardoned.... I'll bear with many in you. Vergl. Forde, *The Witch of Edmonton*, I, 2 (III, p. 194) : My good son,

I'll bear with many faults in thee hereafter ;
Bear thou with mine.

2815 put. Das t ist im Original von der Zeile gefallen ; ebenso das Komma am Ende von 2818.

2847 ff. : place == the court, wo das Kämpfen etc. verboten war.

2854 lies : will.

2925 d. h. Here's the price of sin : Ill thrift. All loose *etc*?

2960 lies : Question.

2969 ff : stand.... stiffe. Wie Shaparoon's Antwort obscön. Vergl. Forde, *Love's Sacrif.* II, 2, wo Mauruccio sagt : I am stiff and strong, während Giacopo bei Seite sagt ; A radish root is a spear of steel in comparison of I know what.

2981 proctor.... consistory. Was Forde's Lebensumstände betrifft, so wissen wir bis jetzt nur, dass er Jurist war ; in welcher Eigenschaft er sich jedoch als solcher betätigte ist unbekannt. Auf Grund der obigen Stelle und der folgenden Zusammenstellung möchte ich annehmen, dass er irgendwie mit dem *consistory court* [1]), einem der *ecclesiastical courts*, in Verbindung zu bringen ist.

I. *The Sun's Darling* I, 1 : In any court, father bald-pate, where my grannam the Moon shows her horns, except the *Consistory Court*; and there she need not appear, *cuckolds* carry such sharp stilettos in their foreheads.

II. *The Fancies*, II, 1 (II, p. 250) ;

Call not
Thy wickedness thy loss : without my knowledge
Thou sold'st me, and in *open court* protestedst
A pre-contract unto another falsely
To justify a separation.

III. *Love's Sacrifice*, III, 1 (II, p. 55) :

Good my lord,
Reclaim your incredulity : my fault
Proceeds from lawful composition
Of wedlock ; he hath seal'd his oath to mine
To be my husband

IV. *Love's Sacrifice*, III, 1 (II, p. 56) : Petruchio, thou art not wise enough to be a *paritor* (== an inferior officer.... that summoned delinquents to a *spiritual court, l. c.* Anm).

V. *The Lady's Trial.* II, 4 (III, p. 44) :

let me appear
Or mine owne lawyer, or in *open court* ——
Like some forsaken client —— in my suit
Be cast for want of honest plea.

Eine Verbindung Forde's mit dem *consistory court* würde es uns auch verständlich machen, dass er mit geringfügigen Ausnahmen sich Sujets gewählt hat, die in der einen oder anderen Weise der Jurisdiction dieses Hofes unterstanden haben würden[2]). Trotz zahlreicher Umfragen, bei denen ich in liebenswürdigster Weise von Prof. Feuillerat unterstützt wurde, ist es mir bis jetzt nicht gelungen, archivalisches Material zu dieser Frage aufzufinden.

3004 throat...... cut in your own defence *etc*. Einen ähnlichen Juristenwitz verewigt

---

[1]) Von diesem Gerichtshof sagt das NED : Formerly a court of great importance, having jurisdiction in matrimonial cases, questions of divorce..... general ecclesiastical and moral discipline. Er wird daher auch oft als bawdy court bezeichnet.

[2]) [Ich sehe nachträglich, dass schon Bodenstedt, *Shakespeare's Zeitgenossen und ihre Werke*, II, p. XXXII, von Forde gesagt hat : Sein Beruf als Jurist gewährte ihm tiefern Einblick in allerlei unnatürliche Verhältnisse und Verirrungen, wie dergleichen im Leben ja oft genug vorkommen, die er dann psychologisch zu erklären und poetisch darzustellen suchte. Korr. Note].

Forde in *The Sun's Darling*, IV, 1 (III, p. 154) : Nay, if you will kill yourself in your own defence, I'll not be of your jury (weil überhaupt keine Gerichtsverhandlung stattfinden kann).

3011 old huddle ; ziemlich gebräuchliches Schimpfwort ; den Complex huddle and twang kann ich jedoch nicht belegen.

3013 way of all flesh = 1) sterben 2) sich begatten.

3015 cue fast ‹ Bedeutung › wie 2367. Nicht im NED.

3017 promist d. h. während Mopas und Bufo ll 3000 — 3016 sprechen.

3038 lies : Here's.

3062 soul. Über die Seele, ihren Wert und ihr Wesen hat Forde lange nachgedacht, was sich naturgemäss in seinem Vocabular manifestiert (vergl. das Wörterverzeichniss). Vergl. nur *'Tis Pity*, II, 5 (I, p. 148) : Things being thus, a pair of souls are lost ; *Love's Sacr.* II, 4 (II, p. 51) : be record to my soul The justice which I for this folly fear ; *Perk. Warb.* II, 2 (II, p. 143) : 'Tis [sc. der Krieg zwischen den Häusern York und Lancaster] a quarrel T'engage a soul in ; *Witch of Edm.* I, 2 (III, p. 193) :

> Am I become so insensible of losing
> The glory of creation's work, my soul ?

Ich bedaure sehr, dass mir Sir John Davies's Elegie *Of the soule of man, and the immortalitie thereof* nicht zugänglich ist, da sie Forde's Ansichten beeinflusst haben kann, denn Sir John war einer der hervorragendsten Juristen seiner Zeit, wie Forde Mitglied des Middle Temple, und sein Gedicht erlebte von 1599-1622 nicht weniger als fünf Auflagen.

3084 shrill lies : thrill.

3168 bold ; im Original scheint für l ein abgesprungenes langes s gestanden zu haben.

3216 first man. Das NED citiert aus 1883, nach Gresley's *Gloss. Coal Mining* : *First man*, the head butty or coal getter in a stall, who... is responsible for the safety of the men working under him and for the proper working of the coal. Mir ist der Complex vollkommen unbekannt. Es kann daher um so wichtiger sein, dass er bei Forde, *'Tis Pity*, V, 6 (I, p. p. 205) vorkommt :

> Gio. Whose hand gave me this wound ?
> Vas. Mine, sir ; I was your first man : have you enough.

An beiden Stellen etwa : ich bin's der für Dich gesorgt hat. Oder sollen wir einfach wörtlich übersetzen und *The Witch of Edmonton*, III, 1 vergleichen : I am thy first man, sculler ; I go with thee ; ply no other but myself. Dekker, *Satirom.* 1006 : let Sir Adam bee your first man still ist mir auch nicht recht klar.

3222 lies : pawn.

3264 lies : murderous.

3284 oul lies : soul.

3304 so lies : too ? Oder liegt ein Anakoluth vor ?

3360 lies : the mastery.

3426 kills in Curtesie ; doch wohl eine Anspielung auf Heywood's *Woman Killed with Kindness*, wie in Forde's *'Tis Pity*, IV, 3 (I, p. 185) : he will go near to kill my lady with unkindness.

3439 Sachlich vergl. Forde, *'Tis Pity* I, 2 (I, p. 116) : Thou art no equal match for me *etc* ; *ibid* p. 118 : Holding a man so base no match for me.

3456 I'le kneel to thee, as to another nature. Vergl. Forde, *The Fancies*, I, 1 (II, p. 230) : Create me what you please of yours ; do this, You are another nature. *The Sun's Darling* IV, 1 (III, p. 155) : Mistery there, like to another nature, Confects the substance of the choicest fruits.

Wie honour, truth *etc*, fate so nimmt auch das Wort nature in Forde's Wörterbuch eine grosse und z. T. eigentümliche Stelle ein. Vergl. Wörterverzeichniss.

3461 unknown   unconscious.

3500 lies : must.

3523 ff. guard..... Then all the world besides. Vergl. Forde's *Love's Sacr.* IV, 2 (II, 87) : This sword.... Shall guard her from an armed troop of fiends And all the earth beside, wozu man vergl. 3255 : and all the treasures of the earth besides.

3580 lies : Stands ?

3547 bought & sold = verraten und verkauft. Aus Forde vergl. nur *Love's Sacr.* IV, 2 : I fear your life is bought and sold.

3618 lies : loyall.

3639 Did I not tell you so from time to time. Ähnliche Lage und ähnl. Ausdruck bei Forde, *The Fancies* IV, 1 (II, p. 293) : Didst not thou, from time to time, tell me as much.

3649 Mit on beginne neuen Vers.

3662 let this kiss new marry us. Vergl. Forde, *The Broken Heart.* V, 3 (I, p. 3:8) : That I new-marry him whose wife I am. Forde gebraucht das Wort sehr häufig in diesem Sinn ; aus *Queene* vergl. 3815 : to new torment me ; 3448 : Shall new revive my dulnes, wo es ebenso überflüssig ist als in *Perkin Warbeck*, I, 1 (II, p. 120) : but for the upstart duke, the new reviv'd York.... he lives again.

3664 What say ? Vergl. Forde, *'Tis Pity*, II, 6 (I, p. 150) : What say ? why d'ye not speak ?

3686 God a' mercy old Suresby. Citat ? Vergl. Nares, s. v. Suresby.

3692 ff. Die ersten Wörter sind zu lesen : heretofore, but, honest, me, honest, (how-)ere.

3718 loose-bodied das stehende Epitheton für Huren.

3720 wholesom instructions. Vergl. Forde, *Love's Sacrifice* IV, 1 (II, p. 80), wo Mauruccio, der die von Ferentes geschwängerte Morona heiratet, den Rat bekommt : Your only course, I can advise you, is to pass to Naples, and set up a house of carnality.

3760 muschatoes. Zur Umstellung vergl. Middleton. ed. Bullen, VIII, p. 14 : muchatoes ; Dekker, *Works*, IV, p. 192 : Mochatoes.

3818 fin lies : sin.

3835 lies : hearty sorrow.

WÖRTERVERZEICHNISS.

Die fett gedruckten Zahlen verweisen auf die Erläuterungen.

(Gentleman-)Usher 1654, 2079
ginger-bread 2090
gipsonly **124**
girl dissilb. **261**
gleek 1864
go in before 1648, 1650 und **1359**
go the way of all flesh **3013**
go thy way for — 319, 504, 1022 und
   vergl. 2928
go the wrong way = sterben **910**
godfathers 210
good **425**, 1810, 2833

hail-shot vb. **838**
hand vb. **715**
hand, make a sweet h. of 2913 und
   vergl. **166**
hand, make a trim h. of **166**
hearke in your eare 3028
hearts of gold 568
heel **3098**
hey do 58, 3210, 3517
hight 483, 1843, 1982
Hiren **1781**
holland (Stoff) 1771
honor 579, **580**, 839, 1140, 1219, 1395,
   1418, 2164, 2249, (2203), 2385, 2473,
   2497, 2730, 3073, 3349, 3487, 3621,
   3678
hony moon adj. **621**
Hospital boy **99**
hucster 2091
hurle-burly 1607

Indeed, forsooth **881**, 980, 2694, 2989
   und cf. 955
Indeed la 140
inheritance **513**
impostume 1222

jack, black jack 1757
jump vb. **622**

la 1162
la, indeed la 140
lady of the ascendant **352**, 489
leachery and covetousnes go together,
   prov. 2929
likelyhoods 1617
longtayle, cut or l. 2985
loose-bodied **3718**
lord ascendant etc. **352**
luxury **1621**

madder then a march hare, prov. 2944
Mahound 1738
make a sweet hand of 2913 und **166**
make a trim hand of **166**
maligo **1780**
manchet 2099
march hare, madder then, prov. 2944
mark (in the mouth) **767**
maunderer **73**
mawle 159
measures, old m. 1586
merchant **806**
mettall'd, true mettall'd blade 3027
mettall men 3518
mistery 1635
mole-hill 1201
moon calf **273**, 1782
moyle ≈ mule 883
muschatoes **3760**
muscle woman **173**
mystery 1635

napary, napery **1023**
nature 78, 324, 413, 510, 524, 844, 857,
   1184, 1414, 2406, 2445, 2447, 2587,
   3290, **3456**, 3636
needles, Spanish 170
new 3448, **3662**, 3707, 3815
nodles 155

oil of serpents 49
owe vb. 1183, 1285, **2573**, 3290, 3482,
   3660
owlaglasses 157

to pass in before **1359**
passing 1644
phew 469, 701, 1389, 1619
pish 572, 1214, 1771, 1905, 2807, 3147,
   3474
placket **609**
pole ≈ pole und poll **1787**
puppy dogs 2039

quaff 368

rags of the old Regiment 292
resolution ; that is my r. **317**, 1684
resolved, to be r. **393**, 532, 543
rife **14**
rine canters 1714
to rip up **1365**
roughy **63**